"The insight that Georgia so unselfishly renders empowers you to stand firmly in your truth and to reflect upon the series of events in your life that shape who you have become."

JoAnn Jenkins

"There is so much wisdom and insight shared that you can only be inspired."

Lynn Adams

"This book is part memoir, part self-help and served as a reminder for me to love myself a little more."

Kristian J.

Redefining

Her

MY JOURNEY TO
SELF-ACCEPTANCE AND LOVE

Redefining Her is part memoir, part-manifesto that explores resilience, embracing and attaching a different meaning to our experiences, reinventing our life and owning our power. It explores how God uses disruption to unleash the power within us...reversing the untruths that we tell ourselves about who we are and giving us permission to launch into who we are supposed to be. Within these pages I impart some of the rawest and most defining moments of my journey—experiences with childhood afflictions, trauma, toxic relationships, disruption, self-sabotage, lessons learned, and ultimately my transformation to self-acceptance, self-awareness, and love. I share my practical guidepost to redefining our experiences which on the other side will elevate us way beyond what we ever imagined. My story is proof that it is possible for us all to overcome difficulty and to heal from our emotional scars. My hope is that my story will empower you to confidently emerge from the burdens of your past story, shift your perspectives, embrace who you are, and in the process of this unveiling discover that you are more than enough—you always were.

The Redefined *Her* is:

Healed from all the debilitating mental constructs that weigh her down, Empowered for impact and Restored into her authentic self.

Redefining

Her

MY JOURNEY TO
SELF-ACCEPTANCE AND LOVE

GEORGIA WOLFE-SAMUELS

ISBN 978-1-953156-19-8

Printed in the United States of America

Redefining
Her

MY JOURNEY TO
SELF-ACCEPTANCE AND LOVE

I impart within these pages some of the most defining moments of my journey—experiences with childhood afflictions, trauma, toxic relationships, disruption, lessons learned, and ultimately my transformation to self-acceptance, self-awareness, and self-love, with the hope that my story will empower you to confidently emerge from the burdens of your past story, shift your perspectives, embrace who you are, and in the process of this unveiling discover that you are more than enough—you always were.

The Redefined *Her* is:

Healed from all the debilitating mental constructs that weigh her down, Empowered for impact and Restored into her authentic self.

Redefining

Her

**MY JOURNEY TO
SELF-ACCEPTANCE AND LOVE**

For my precious pea,

Moe

You have so enriched my life and have shown me the power of love. You were my God-strength during some of the most difficult times in my life. Thank you for always believing in me. I am grateful and honored to call you my daughter.

For every woman who is on the journey to the best version of themself and who desires to respond and operate at the highest level of contribution.

Dear God,

Thank You for being my continuous source and supply even in moments when I did not believe in You. Thank You for the vision and the provision for the visions. Thank You for the challenges throughout my life for in hindsight I see that they were meant to shape me for my purpose.

"A smooth sea never made a skilled sailor."

Franklin D. Roosevelt

You are the sailor of your life. God is the captain. The ebb and flow of the waves and tides are the power to your purpose.

"The foundational base of redefining Her is rooted in what She believes about Her core self. The first step in redefining Her is knowing at Her core that She is worth it."

Georgia Wolfe-Samuels

Table of Contents

Introduction

"Internal impressions, if not aligned, falsely defines us."

Georgia Wolfe-Samuels

I am ... because He is! Oftentimes what comes after "I am" is dictated by our outside world, the people around us—whether it be family or friends, or the lies we tell ourselves. Too often "I am" is influenced by the color of our skin, the color, texture, or length of our hair, our physical curves or lack thereof, the features of our physical being or our economic circumstances. But "I am" has nothing to do with the world around us and everything to do with who created us. On purpose. For His will.

For most of my life, the words that followed "I am" were influenced by my negative experiences: abandonment, poverty, sexual abuse, financial, verbal and emotional abuse, domestic violence, miscarriages ... all defined me. But what had the most profound impact on how I showed up was the lie I told myself as a little five-year-old girl (I'll tell you all about it later). That lie subconsciously infiltrated my entire being and impacted not only the lens in which I viewed the world but also the lens in which I viewed myself. The traumas that came after reinforced what I had already internalized: I am unworthy. I am not enough.

In my journey to define "I am," I first had to find Whose I am. As if He was lost! In hindsight, He was there all along, carrying me through every journey (the joyful and the painful). But until I tweaked the lens through which I viewed my external and internal worlds, I would not recognize Him. The "I" is intentional because it required work on my part, and it will take work on your part too. I had to own my story; this book is meant to cement it in history. I had to take the first step, even when the subsequent steps were not visible. I had to forgive myself and continue to exercise grace. In the words of one of my favorite authors, Brene Brown, *"[o]wning our story can be hard but not nearly as difficult as spending our lives running from it...Only when we are brave enough to explore the darkness will we discover the infinite power of our light."*

There is light in each of us! I uncovered my light. I am telling my story—a story that is still being written. But unlike the first 40 chapters, I am and will be fully present, purposed, and poised to do His will. My story is not one of victimhood. Instead, it is one of survivorship, of soaring despite the odds. A story of resiliency, of finding the gems in my journey. I offer the gems in my journey in hopes that it will help you to find the gems in yours. That it will change some of the damaging narratives you may have grown up with: devalued, unworthy, not enough. My hope is that my story will propel you to elevate your understanding of who and Whose you are and spark an internal rebellion or an internal awakening to show up as the highest and best version of yourself—confident and fully able.

Disclaimer

Some names and identifying details have been
changed to protect the privacy of individuals.

PART I

PART I

Peeling Back the Layers

"The most powerful message is the one that you tell yourself."

Georgia Wolfe-Samuels

PART I

Peeling Back the Layers

"Face the Past, Heal the Future"

Van Jones

Introspection can be one of the most challenging processes in life. I used to wish my life came with a reset button, especially the ugly parts that have caused me shame, pain, and grief. My childhood was not picturesque. Neither was my adolescence, or my early adult years for that matter. In fact, it was not until age forty amid my disruption (discussed in Part II … keep reading) when the lens through which I saw my world changed. Prior to this process, there were experiences that when interpreted formed the core of my belief system of how I viewed myself, and which contributed to my unhealthy life cycles. The journey to self-love and accepting myself despite my flaws required me to face some hard truths and lies I told myself about myself.

Thankfully, I have come to realize that I am where I am and I am who I am because of my journey, and that God was in my story all along, even when I did not believe in His existence. God's plan is not a "quick fix" plan. He is intentional. He is patient. You will need patience. His process is one of eternal transformation as He, surely in His time, unveils His power within us, and who He created us to be, removing the veils of our false sense of self whether self-inflicted or inflicted on us by others.

While the following pages illustrate the tapestry of my personal journey to the root of my becoming, the challenges are not unique to me. God is in your story as well. There is wisdom in your wounds.

Chapter One

Self-Sabotage
The Personal Lie

"Take a day to heal from the lies you have told yourself
and the ones that have been told to you."

Maya Angelou

Self-Sabotage – the personal lie is the tale we tell ourselves about who we are and what we deserve and don't deserve in life. It is an inaccurate belief or perspective that disaffirms our intrinsic sense of worth—shame, anger, unworthiness—resulting in the outer manifestation of these inner feelings in the form of unhealthy behaviors or limiting thought patterns. Whatever the form, self-sabotage always diminishes the passion and energy we need to achieve our goals, fulfill our dreams, and to respond to the world in **POWER** (Perspectives. Optimism. Wisdom. Empathy. Respect.).

The Mother Wound

I was the youngest of two daughters for my father and the youngest of six children for my mother (four sisters, three of which I knew nothing about until age 17, and one brother). I grew up in Jamaica, West Indies for the first eleven years of my life before migrating to New York in December 1990. Nine years prior, my mother migrated to the United States, unknown to my father while he was at work. She took me with her initially, from what I came to understand was a brief moment before sending me back on a plane to Jamaica. I don't recall speaking to or seeing my mother again until maybe age five (could have been earlier) when my father and I showed up a day late for what was either my maternal grandfather or grandmother's funeral in the countryside of St. Elizabeth, Jamaica. I never knew my maternal grandparents.

My mom was scheduled to depart back to the States the next morning. I recall sitting on the edge of the bed in the guest room where she stayed, looking at her in awe while she dressed and packed in preparation for her departure to the airport. She was beautiful. She was tall and slender, with caramel-toned skin, features I did not possess. I took notice. It made an impression. As she walked toward the mirror, she removed the pink curlers from her hair and began brushing the thick, bouncy curls of her shoulder-length hair, which was highlighted with streaks of bronze. Later in life, I would learn that she was a hairdresser by profession. I admired her intensely in that moment in an attempt to capture everything I could in the event I did not see her again. I was fascinated by her beauty. She brushed her hair with a silver antique brush, to which the matching comb and mirror lay on the dresser to her left. I was sad that she was leaving. Back then I longed for her, which was maybe why I asked her if she would leave with me the antique brush and comb set she was using (that was after I already asked her if I could go home with her). She responded with a resounding "no" before offering me a travel-size bottle of Keri lotion as a replacement. Another impression was made. Some thirty-five years later, it would be revealed that it was at this moment that Half-Pint me was born—when I first told myself the lie—I was not worthy; my mother was leaving—again without me, because I was not enough. My skin was not caramel-toned, and I did not have long, beautiful bouncy hair like she did, and therefore I was not beautiful. This is my first memory of her and would be the last time I saw her until I was 23 years old and a college student in New York. Not hearing from or seeing my mother for another eighteen years solidified this lie. The childhood traumas that followed further reinforced this lie. Half-Pint me, was the version of me that operated and responded from a tenet of fear, unworthiness and the belief that I just was not enough. Subconsciously, this experience formed the core of my self-belief and influenced the cycle of choices I would make throughout my life, including my relationship with God—that is until The Disruption.

I often hear that in the early years of a child's life, their brain is like a sponge, keenly absorbing all the information around them. These formative years establish the foundation of their personality and self-confidence. In the words of my dear Pastor Dennis Rouse, "children are very good receptors but very bad interpreters." Children are considered bad interpreters because they lack the experiences and the wisdom to analyze events or situations. As a result, there is the risk of false interpretations.

In my personal story, the issue here was not the event of my mother telling me "no" or her leaving me. Instead, the issue was my interpretation of why she told me "no" and my interpretation of why she was not a tangible part of my life. Maybe the brush and comb were sentimental to my mother, which influenced why she could not part with them. Or maybe she was just not the nurturing type. Whatever the reason, it really did not matter. What mattered was how I internalized this experience. I interpreted my mother's absence to mean that I was not worthy to be loved. For years I longed for her, that she would visit, call, or write. I would frequently wish that my hair was like hers and daydreamed of her brushing my hair (looking back, this was the reason I continuously prodded my father for a perm until I finally got one at around age nine). Yearning turned into anger, not directed at my mother but instead at God. While at the time I was not a regular attendee at church (unless I was at my paternal sister's house where we were forced every Sunday to drink our porridge and attend Mount Carmel Baptist church), I heard of the Divine, but I did not have a personal relationship with Him. In fact, I impressed upon myself that if He did in fact exist, He did not love me. For if He did, He would not allow me to feel the pain I was feeling as a symptom to my mom's abandonment and from my dad's resulting anger. As a result of this thought process, nothing I did was ever good enough, a perception that lingered into my adult years as I continuously felt that I had to be more and do more in an effort to be considered worthy, but never quite getting there. Graduating from high school with honors a semester early was not good enough. Graduating from college and going to work for one of the world's top accounting firms (an offer I received in my junior year of college) was not good enough. Passing all four parts of the CPA exam in the first sitting was not good enough. Mind you, this was back in the day when the exam was all manual and not the computerized version administered today. Being brave to leave with my baby in tow from a tumultuous relationship laced with physical violence was not good enough. Purchasing my first home at age thirty while being single and a divorced mother was not good enough. Publishing my first book at age thirty-one was not good enough. Career promotions were not good enough. It was a continuous cycle of achieving but still not being good enough.

Changing my Lens

When I look back at my childhood some thirty-six years later, in particular that day in the guest room with my mother, it is apparent the profound impact that one event with my mother shaped my core beliefs about myself, the corresponding impact those beliefs had on how I showed up in and responded to the world, and the coping tactics I concocted to survive. Internal perceptions of unworthiness and not being enough influenced the relationships I chose to be in and stay in even when toxic. I meandered through life subconsciously with a poor self-image. I showed up at work unconfident, afraid to raise my hands for the challenging and sometimes also the easy projects because I did not feel confident in my abilities (despite my prior achievements), and feared the spotlight would highlight my imagined, fictitious and false disqualifications. In my relationships I was insecure and felt undeserving of true healthy love. I accepted bad behaviors and failed to establish safe boundaries. My coping tactics included shopping (a whole lot of it), busyness, sometimes isolation/withdrawal, and avoiding disappointment by refusing to be vulnerable or dependent on anyone outside of myself (I still struggle with this).

Despite my mother's absence, I am grateful to her for being the vessel through which I came into the world. I often wondered what invaluable life lessons I could have learned from her, how she could have prepared me for motherhood, what fashion sense she could have relayed as I struggled to find mine (especially in my teen and early adulthood years). I guess at this point I may never know. Our relationship never recovered, but I am open to the possibility. I was hopeful at age 23 when, while I was still in college I would send her money periodically to help her with her expenses. By this point she was back living in Jamaica. However, that relationship severed once she colluded with what I believe was a fake doctor to con me out of thousands of dollars for medical bills he could not produce and lamely tried to explain.

Choosing our parents is not an option. Knowing this gives me comfort that maybe she fulfilled her purpose (as it relates to me), maybe she was only meant to be the vessel through which I entered this world. Changing my lens required tuning into the words of God and defining myself how He defined me, *fearfully and wonderfully made (Psalms 139:14)*. It required vulnerability. It required forgiveness. It required introspection on the root cause as opposed to the fruits of my issues. Only the manufacturer could fix my thoughts but not before completely disrupting my life.

Pause † Reflect

The Big Lie:

- You are defined by your negative experiences or negative thoughts.
- You are who others say you are (including your caretakers).
- You are of no value because of your past mistakes or your flaws.
- You are not enough.
- You will never achieve your heart's desires or your dreams.

Truth:

- You are who God says you are.
- You matter, created by God for a specific purpose.
- You are more than enough regardless of your:
    - Size
    - Imperfections
    - Weight
    - Culture (including family culture)
    - Mistakes
    - Experiences

- You are more than enough just as you are and while in progress to your greatest self.

- You will achieve whatever you set your mind to and what is within God's purpose for you.

To make significant progress to the wholehearted you, it is essential to identify how your inner saboteur is operating in your life.

Self-Sabotage is simply a coping mechanism, the actions we take to fill an often unconscious need, often preventing us from true joy and living in our purpose. Make a list of specific habits, behaviors, emotional trends, or thoughts you have about yourself to sabotage yourself. Give yourself permission to be ruthlessly honest. As you complete this exercise, please keep in mind that in order to show up as your best self, from a place of authentic wholeness, it is essential that you are authentically you, flaws and all. All you. This will require you to eradicate all that is not authentically you. As you make this list, create action steps, practices or tasks that you will pursue to eradicate the thought or stop that action. Please be patient with and extend yourself grace, as this process takes time.

_____

_____

_____

_____

_____

_____

_____

_____

_____

_____

_____

_____

Chapter Two

Molded By Childhood Impressions

"Children are like wet cement:
whatever falls on them makes an impression."

Haim Ginott

Parents and caretakers have a tremendous power in molding a child's becoming. With no accompanying manual, and back in my day no internet or Google research for a guide, this can be an overwhelming task. Nonetheless, as parents and caretakers we are responsible for instilling in our children a foundation of values on which their future lives will be built.

A Bedrock Is A Solid Foundation

My father was a single father for the entire duration of my childhood (not counting his various girlfriends). We moved various times throughout Kingston, Jamaica before moving to Hellshire, St. Catherine when I was about age eight. My father had acquired a mortgage to build his dream home where we resided together until my father migrated to the United States right after hurricane Gilbert devastated Jamaica in September 1988. Prior to the hurricane, the house was not quite complete but had the basic four walls, two bedrooms, a kitchen, living and dining room combo, one bathroom, tiled flooring throughout, and a zinc roof. The walls of the exterior and interior were bare concrete, not yet painted to give it the vibrance it longed for. My father had vast plans for the house, which included finishing the veranda and a cellar to hide in times of natural disasters. The unfinished cellar was our saving grace during Hurricane Gilbert. It was common in Jamaica for your home to be in a continuous construction phase for long periods of time as a common aspiration among almost every Jamaican is to become a homeowner. However, due to lack of funding in most cases, it requires us to start small and build upwards, a plan that requires a great deal of patience and a whole lot of discipline—discipline was the system of governance throughout the Jamaican culture. In fact, if as a child you were believed to be out of line, and your parents were not around, a neighbor, teacher, or other grownup had full permission to discipline you, and if you ever thought about telling your parents, you had another spanking coming!

Life Wounds

"Young lady, come back here and say good afternoon to Mr. Glen! *Mi sure seh mi teach you manners!*" That was the command from my father as I entered the back gate to the yard of our home in Hellshire, on my way home from school, and proceeded to pass my father and Glen in the backyard. My father was in the process of pointing out to Glen something on the house that he wanted fixed. I had acknowledged my father but intentionally ignored Glen as I passed by. Glen was a distant neighbor who my father often hired to do odd jobs around the house. In fact, it was for this reason that Glen had the keys to our house and why earlier that year I found myself inside Glen's home to retrieve the keys to access my house. I was around nine years old. I was wearing a blue and white jogging suit that I had been gifted for my birthday. That day, I stood at Glen's front door calling Rohan, Glen's stepson and my friend. Rohan was a couple years older than me. Glen, who was in the house, responded that Rohan was in the back and to "come on in." He lied. Once I entered the house, Glen then appeared behind me and closed and locked the front door. He told me to have a seat, to which I obliged. I had no idea what was coming next. He told me that Rohan had the keys and that he should be back from the store shortly and that in the meantime he would teach me how to play a card game to pass time. Something did not feel right; he had just told me Rohan was in the backyard! The game of his choice was *Go Fish*. This game entails collecting sets of four cards of the same rank by asking other players for cards you think they may have of a particular rank. If the player asked does not have any cards of the requested rank, they say, "Go fish." The player asking must then retrieve the top card from the undealt deck of cards, in hopes that it matches the rank the player seeks. If the drawn card is the rank requested, the player asking gets another turn. Once the cards run out, whoever collects the most books of cards from the same rank wins the game. Glen, however, had a planned twist to this game, as he disturbingly suggested that the winner would get to remove the loser's clothes. I lost the game. I refused to get undressed. As Glen grabbed me and attempted to take my clothes off to claim his prize, I fought tirelessly to escape his grasp and his attempt to take away my innocence. I grabbed a huge figurine of a rooster sitting on the center table and slammed it against his arm... this was my moment to escape. I ran toward the back door, which was obviously open based on the light that was being reflected into the living room. The back door was about five feet from the ground level, and since the house was still under construction as many homes in the neighborhood were at that time, there were no stairs connecting the back door to the backyard. Nonetheless, I jumped down to the platform and ran to my neighbor's house and stayed there until later that night when my father came looking for me. I told my father what happened that day and why I could not come home. I am not sure what my father did, if anything. But his command to acknowledge Glen as I entered the back gate to our house that day and the mere fact that he continued to hire Glen for odd jobs was evidence that he did not do enough. Another impression was planted—I was not worthy of protection. Needless to say, every opportunity Glen had to touch me inappropriately after that incident, he did. This was my first defining life wound.

From a Father Figure to an Abuser

My father migrated to New York a couple weeks after hurricane Gilbert ravished our home and many parts of the island of Jamaica in September 1988. I was left in the care of my aunts, but was periodically rotated between my aunts, godmother, and stepmother's homes. During the summer of 1990, my Aunt

Paulette, my father's youngest sister who at the time resided in Kingston with her son's father Troy, was in need of a babysitter to watch their baby son. I was "voluntold" to go, and for a couple weeks resided in the home they shared while they went to work. I looked up to Troy. He was an electrician at the time and would often stop by my Aunt Sonia's house while I resided with her, always a bearer of gifts ranging from candy to ice cream and sometimes cash. In fact, my first experience at a movie theater was gifted from Troy, who had a contract with The Carib theater. He took my little cousin and I, and we watched a movie while he worked. I knew him for years. I trusted him. But he would eventually betray that trust. He violated me during the night while my aunt slept. I woke up to an excruciating pain as Troy, who I estimate was about 300 pounds at the time, penetrated me. He covered my mouth with one hand, pressing my head into the pillow while using the weight of his body to keep me in position. My aunt snored loudly in the background. The baby was sound asleep. I was terrified! The next morning, Troy handed me some money which I guess was supposed to be payoff for my silence. I don't recall the amount. I took the money and used it to pay my bus fare to my Aunt Sonia's place of employment at the NBC Bank in Half Way Tree, Kingston the next day. As I entered the bank where she worked, I proceeded to the ladies' room where I saw a couple of her co-workers and who I asked to tell my aunt I was in the bathroom. I told my Aunt Sonia what happened in that moment and that I was not going back to Aunt Paulette's house. I learned later that Aunt Paulette blamed me and accused me of wanting her man. I never spoke to my Aunt Paulette again, not even twenty-eight years later when we encountered each other at my paternal grandfather's funeral.

I never bothered telling my father, who was residing in New York at the time, about this incident because I did not feel it would matter to him. After all, look how he'd handled the incident with Glen. Years later, after migrating to New York, my father overheard a conversation between my sister and I as we discussed not wanting to attend Thanksgiving at my Aunt Sonia's house, who by this time had migrated to New York as well and was residing in Brooklyn. I had learned through Aunt Sonia that Troy was an invited guest. My paternal sister, who has always been and still remains my confidant, conspired with me to play sick so that we would not have to attend Thanksgiving dinner. My father appeared shocked at this revelation at the time, but a few days later told me that he'd spoken with Aunt Sonia, who noted that she had spoken to my Aunt Paulette at the time of the "alleged" incident, and that she had denied anything happened. He took their words over mine. Unfortunately, I was not shocked. This reaffirmed my then belief that I was unworthy and therefore not worthy of protection.

My Earthly Father

My childhood was lost. In the years following my encounters with sexual violence, there was a continuous storm brewing inside of me, spiraling into anger and resentment. The relationship with my earthly father was broken for a combination of reasons, but primarily because of how the situations with Glen and Troy were handled, which resulted in a lack of trust for my father. But the relationship with my father was on a downward spiral prior to and in between these traumatic incidents. Over the years, he would have girlfriends, some of whom did not care too much for me or my sister. My father would often put our needs secondary to the needs of whatever girlfriend was in the picture at the time. I recall a time in my early childhood when my father's girlfriend Olivia and her daughter Yanique were spending the night at our house. Yanique and I were sharing my bed, and Olivia and my father were sharing his. It was a stormy night, and Yanique was in a deep sleep. I, on the other hand, was scared. The strong wind cast a shadow from the trees outside onto the glass panes of my bedroom window. Naturally I was scared and would repeatedly run to my father's bed, to which he responded over and over again by walking me back to my own bed. I did this several times throughout the night. Apparently, my repeated journey back to his room became a problem for my father and Olivia because shortly after she stormed out in the middle of the night and in the middle of the storm to walk home. My father was furious with me and scolded that if anything happened to her it would be my fault. Another impression—I was a burden.

And then there was Darcia, the other girlfriend who forced me to stand in a fire ants' nest as punishment because I did not clean the refrigerator properly. During that same encounter, she also punished my sister, who was visiting at the time, by hitting her in her back. Once my father came home from work and was debriefed of the incident, he did nothing. However, days later once my sister went back to her home and told her mother about the incident, all hell broke loose because Mama Claire came in beast mode. Darcia must have gotten wind that she was coming because as Mama Claire entered the back door, she went through the front door and ran up the street. Mama Claire did not catch her that day, but boy I secretly wished I could have seen that beatdown (this was before Mama Claire got saved). Mama Claire stayed around until my dad came home and boy, did she lash out at him. I can't remember all that Mama Claire said to my father that day in the heat of the moment, but what stood out for me was (in patios) *"If any a yuh woman eva put dem han pan mi dawta again, mi ago buss dem ass so u betta tell dem seh nuh touch mi pickney."* Another impression—I had no one to stand up for me.

Research tells us that a positive father-daughter relationship can have a huge impact on a young girl's life and even determine whether she develops into a confident woman. A father's influence in his daughter's life shapes her self-esteem, her self-image, her confidence, and her opinions of men. The then tumultuous relationship with my father directly influenced the value I placed in myself or the lack thereof, and the type of relationships I entered and stayed in. Our relationship worsened as I entered my hormonal years and would be tested from time to time. He would often state that he did not want any more children, that it was my mother who wanted another child and now he was stuck with me since my mother left. These words would sink in and would rise to the forefront of my mind whenever I would attempt to do anything that required even an ounce of confidence. Over the years, our relationship continued to spiral downhill to the point where we were not on speaking terms from my second semester in college and throughout my college experience.

While my childhood was clearly not idyllic, to better understand myself and who God created me to be, I had to come face to face with my past and seek a deeper understanding of my story. Clearly there was sorrow there, but within it there was also glory. At times, I used to wish my life came with a reset button. Oftentimes I wanted to change my story, my struggles, my family dynamics, my physical features because perhaps if I looked different, then my circumstances may have turned out differently. It has been a journey of intense pain. But God was there all along. In fact, He was present in the form of my high school guidance counselor, Mr. Ray Serina. Mr. Serina was a short, witty, white man with a receding hairline who would dress in the best two-piece suits daily as if he was working in an investment bank on Wall Street. I came on Mr. Serina's radar because of my declining school grades. He summoned me to his office, as any guidance counselor who cares about their students would. His office became my safe space for the duration of my high school experience. He would talk to me about creating my career goals and would help me plot out the steps and classes I needed to take to achieve those goals. When his attempt to engage my father in discussions or concerns on how I was progressing failed, he took me under his wing. I would visit his office daily, whether it was to plead my case for release from my regent level calculus class he was forcing me to take because it was just too hard, or to just cry because something happened at home that triggered my sorrow. He would always make time to talk to me, and would always push me beyond my self-inflicted limits. He was the sounding ear and my comfort when at sixteen years old I struggled with suicidal thoughts. He funded my first pair of eyeglasses and paid the corresponding optometrist bill when at age fifteen I had difficulty seeing the classroom board from my assigned seating, somewhere in the middle of the class. He reviewed and paid for all my college applications and reviewed and critiqued my application essays to ensure I was putting my best foot forward. Mr. Serina had a profound and positive impact on my life in the midst of my gloom, and for that I would be forever grateful. Mr Serina believed in me at a time when I did not believe in myself.

I would often ask why God allowed the negative experiences I encountered to happen? The answer that resonated with me came via a '80's Peloton cycling class workout in my basement with instructor Hannah Corbin—"God gave you the mountain to show others it can be moved." The glory in my childhood experiences is that they made me the strong woman I am today, physically, mentally and spiritually. My journey of becoming required forgiveness (the most difficult of which was forgiving my father), mercy (for myself and others), self-love (a daily ritual), and healing. My experiences, a portion of which is exhibited in this book, were on the job training for my purpose. This work is in no way meant to critique my mother or father because they may have done the best that they could at the time. After all, I have no knowledge of what they endured as children or how those experiences affected the way they parented. Instead, this book is meant to provide clarity on the experiences that shaped who I thought I was and how I came to understand and embrace who I am, with hope that my story will inspire the transformation in others.

Pause † Reflect

- Our greatest pain is often linked to our caretakers. Pain from our caretakers is believed to have the most impact because our caretakers are tasked with establishing the foundation of who we are. With God's mercy we can overcome.

- Oftentimes our caretakers are not equipped to provide the nurturing we need to establish a firm and positive foundation in who we are because they themselves have not healed from their experiences. Grant them grace.

- Our parents were chosen for us. We had no input in that decision. Any resulting pain from your childhood grooming, while not God's intent to harm us, should not be our fortress, but instead He will use it as fuel for our purpose. Forgive them.

Chapter Three

The Raging Storm

"And then one day, the storm ran out of rain."

Georgia Wolfe-Samuels

At birth, the human infant has no sense of self. Our sense of self is developed gradually over time and is strongly influenced from our interactions with our culture, the most influential of which are our parents and caretakers. How we perceive ourselves is largely based on how we were programmed to see ourselves. Our childhoods are meant to be the wonder years of our journey. They are supposed to be carefree, meant for exploring and learning. About our surroundings. About us. They are meant to be reckless and curious. Not to be encumbered by heavy adult experiences we are not yet trained to maneuver. These formative years form our foundational belief system, coloring the rest of our lives, our internal and external landscape, and ultimately our identity. That is until He changes our lenses.

Our perception of our identity is the engine that propels us along our life journey. It influences our relationships with others and ourselves. Our self-perception is created by the fusing of various external and internal inputs and influences throughout our life, including our experiences, our care-takers' belief system, family culture, other people's opinions, etcetera. If our identity is broken, we are broken. If it is incorrectly defined, then the wrong definition of who we are colors our story. The lie we tell ourselves about ourselves or that others inflicted upon us becomes the law by which we are governed and influences our mental and outward habits. Our habits then dictate the quality of our lives. Childhood wounds of not belonging, constantly moving from relative to relative, unhealed wounds from the relationship with my mother, my father, and the men that sexually abused me for a long time defined me, colored my perceptions, and fueled how I showed up every day. Racial intolerance did not make it any easier.

As a young black girl, I migrated to the US at around age eleven, settling in the boroughs of the Bronx. Shortly after the move, violence erupted in Los Angeles in March of 1991 in response to the savage beating of Rodney King, a black man brutally beaten by police. For months, the news was swarmed with information of the resulting case against the respective officers charged and their subsequent acquittal. The country was in chaos. I was constantly bombarded with images and languages dehumanizing us of a darker complexion. It was my first time being exposed to racism. I was confused. This is not to say our cultural interactions back home in Jamaica were free of conflict, for we had our own share of prejudice (against Rastafarianism, economic segregation, colorism, etc). But here I was moving from a country where our motto was "Out of Many, One People" and now living in a country where we were perceived as three-fifths human merely because of the color of our skin. Can you imagine what this experience did to a little girl who was already out of tune with who she was! Not only was she feeling unworthy within the confines of her family, but she was now living within a larger society where she or anyone that looked like her did not matter. We were viewed as unworthy because of the color of our skin.

Deep in My Roots

I was nineteen years old when I met my ex-husband and my daughter's father. I was a junior in college at the time. He was a friend of my then-hairdresser and was our designated ride to a Caribbean Boat Ride Party, scheduled to depart from New Rochelle, New York in the summer of 1998. He was older, ten years my senior to be exact. He had the sexiest brown eyes and the most captivating smile. He pursued me, and I was smitten. I was desperate for connection, and he provided the attention I'd too long craved. We were inseparable that first day and for the days that followed our connection. Months later, I would find out during a conversation with his sister that he was married and that the place we spent many nights was not his primary place of residence. Our relationship hit a sudden pause. We reconnected two and a half years later when I exited another failed relationship that involved two miscarriages, infidelity, and a failed engagement. He was there for moral support. He was also going through a divorce, and we bonded as a source of support for each other.

A year later, I became pregnant with our daughter Monique, and we made the decision to combine our households. A couple months into playing house, our relationship took a downhill turn, with the first physical blow materializing just when I was about three months pregnant with our daughter.

It was a chilly Saturday afternoon in December of 2002. I was still perplexed and deeply bothered from the events of the night before. I'd worked late the night prior in an effort to finalize a project to meet the fast approaching deadlines. Had I not finalized the project that night, it meant I would have to work over the weekend to meet the deadline the following Monday. Considering that it was approaching wintertime in New York, which meant it was cold, I was pregnant and working later than usual, I thought it sensible that the father of my child would want to pick me up from work as opposed to me taking the hour-long subway ride home to the Bronx. However, the phone call to make my request was a bit suspicious—for one, his answer was that he would not be able to make it but he could not specify why. Additionally, any further conversations were muted as if he was in the presence of someone he did not want to know I was on the phone or that he did not want me to know he was in the presence of. To make matters worse, he had the audacity to come home at 7 am on that Saturday morning! Not wanting to be stressed out (I had two miscarriages before and wanted to minimize the possibility of another one. Furthermore, my pregnancy was already considered high risk), I left that morning to go to Mama Claire's house (my bonus mother's house who by this point was also now living in New York) to get my thoughts together. Later that Saturday afternoon, while I was still at Mama Claire's house, I received a phone call from my daughter's father asking what I was cooking for his dinner, to which I saltily replied that I was not his maid. The background noise indicated he was driving and had one of his best friends with him in the car. I was on speaker phone. He paused, which indicated he was not pleased with my response. Later that afternoon, as I entered the front door to our apartment, it was clear that some drama was about to unfold as my daughter's father approached me and pushed me against the wall, holding me there in a choke hold while simultaneously screaming that I had disrespected him earlier in front of his friend. His friend, who was also there in the apartment, approached us in an attempt to calm him down and release the grip he had on me, continuously reminding him that I was pregnant. He ignored him and proceeded to drag me by my neck into our bedroom down the hall, slamming and locking the door behind us. While in the room, he held me in a headlock position with his left hand while simultaneously pounding my head with his right fist, the result of which was a huge swelling to my head and severe abdominal pain. With each blow all I could think about was my unborn child—there was just no way he or she would survive this assault. I had to fight to save my baby! In pursuit of fighting back, I descended my teeth into the topside of his left wrist, resulting in bleeding and a wound that would remind him of that day every time he attempts to put on a watch. As he released the chokehold, I ran out the bedroom and down the hall towards the kitchen, grabbed the house phone, and dialed 911 before he would catch up to me. A few minutes later, when the police appeared at our apartment door, it would turn out that I was the one they wanted to take to jail because he was bleeding and I was not! I lost faith in the police that day. I felt defeated.

But this was not the first sign of abuse. In fact , prior to the physical abuse there were so many red flags that I failed to acknowledge as warning signs of the devastation that was to come. I misinterpreted his insecurities to be love. His constant chastising of me and frequent accusations when it came to my male co-workers, and even my brother, who according to him, we were too close to just be siblings, were all mistakenly interpreted to mean that he was fearful of losing me, which must have meant that he really did love me. That narrative was completely false.

Existing versus Living

At the point when my daughter Monique was born, I was in my second year at one of the top accounting firms in the world. To the naked eye, it would appear that I had it all together—a great career, a handsome and talented partner, and a beautiful bouncing baby girl. My relationship with God, however, was non-existent. I had grown to acknowledge that God existed, but I certainly did not have a relationship with Him. In fact, my thought process was *Hey I am not a liar, thief, or murderer,* and as long as I did not wear any of those labels I was good. I had no idea what I was missing out on not being in a direct relationship with Him. I was a functional self-diagnosed depressive, visiting psychologist after psychologist in an attempt to figure out the non-existing relationship with my mother and at the time the halted relationship with my father, who I did not reconnect with until shortly after my daughter's birth. At this point I had not spoken to my father in years since he threw my sister and me out of the house for the second time at age 18. I felt alone, with no clue of who I really was. Despite my accomplishments, I felt disconnected from the world.

It was my attempt to keep the appearance of having it all together when I decided to say yes to a move to Atlanta, Georgia at the request of my daughter's father, and began the process of a request for a job transfer. A move that was partially influenced by the September 11th attacks on the United States of America and the corresponding vulnerability of the state of New York, in addition to the statewide blackout that occurred in 2003 when Monique was just a few months old. The 2003 New York statewide blackout was too much a reminder of the September 11th attack. I was hoping the move to Atlanta would provide a better quality of life for our daughter and improve my relationship with her father. Three weeks after submitting my request for a transfer, we were packed and on our way to Atlanta.

The drive to Atlanta from New York was approximately fifteen hours, arriving in the pitch of the night. My daughter's father drove the U-Haul with his son and all our belongings while I drove in our sedan driven by a female friend of ours along with baby Monique and my father. Upon arrival at the apartment complex we planned to call home until we found a house to purchase, I along with our female friend decided to drive to the nearest Walmart to purchase baby supplies, a kettle to warm some water to make the baby's milk (there was no planned unpacking of the truck until the next morning) and food for us all to eat. Between finding the Walmart (this is before the days of the map equipped smartphone and our car was not equipped with a navigation system) and the long checkout lines, it took us a couple hours to get back to the apartment with food and supplies in hand. Upon our arrival back to the apartment, it was clear that my daughter's father was upset and as I would find out later, he believed I left with his female friend to visit another man, specifically my fictional boyfriend. Because we had house guests, specifically my father, his twisted thoughts did not escalate into a physical blowout until a week later when there were no guests present. This was the second time he physically laid hands on me, and unfortunately it wasn't the last. Here I was in a new state, no friends or family for at least 800 miles. I was embarrassed, bruised, and confused. It was still pretty warm in Atlanta, but to hide my bruises specifically from my new coworkers, I had to wear long sleeves and pretend my body and my mind were not in complete disarray.

Our relationship continued this way for another year with periodic episodes of emotional, financial, verbal, and physical assaults, including his threats to kill me and leave our daughter motherless. Over time I stopped calling my sisters, who I historically spoke to on a daily basis. I became reserved and distant from family, friends, and even my new co-workers. I also lost a lot of weight as eating was not on my list of priorities. I felt hopeless, defeated, and unworthy of a healthy and loving relationship which is probably why I decided to marry him shortly after moving to Atlanta. I felt a pervasive numbness throughout my body consistently. I was merely existing versus living.

When Enough is Enough

It was a Sunday morning in the middle of August, 2004. It was now two months since I had given my life to Christ and was in the process of building a personal relationship with Him. That morning as I prepared breakfast before getting ready for church, my ex-husband began behaving erratically, hurling swears at me, yelling that I was the worst thing that had ever happened to him. This continued as I showered and prepared for church and even escalated to him kicking the bathroom door off the hinges while I showered. I tried my best to remain calm and as I attempted to get my baby Monique dressed, he snatched her from my arms and said she was not leaving with me. I continued to get dressed, extremely fearful whether I was going to make it out the house.

Well, I did, and as I approached my car, I heard a hissing noise from my back tire—my tire had a punched hole in it. I drove to PepBoys to get my tire fixed and later that afternoon returned to the apartment with the intent to figure out a strategy to take Monique and leave. For good. Upon entering the apartment, the verbal assaults reignited, and as I picked up my baby, he snatched the prescription glasses off my face, breaking them in pieces. A tug of war ensued between us. He eventually snatched my phone and the baby. I was able to escape without Monique and, relying on a pair of prescription shades I had in the car, was able to drive away. I stayed in a motel that night, scared and confused what to do next.

Early the next morning, I woke up to a phone call from the front desk—he'd found out which motel I was staying at through his friend, who I had called the night before to vent. My ex-husband had to go to work and had nowhere to leave Monique—at least that was his rationale to getting the front desk clerk to call my room at 5 in the morning. I got dressed and walked out to the front desk and took my baby. I had her now, and that was all that mattered. Later that morning, I took her to her babysitter, letting her know not to release Monique to anyone as I was going to the house to get some clothes and my personal documents and would come right back for her. I arrived at the apartment and climbed the stairs to the second floor where our apartment was located. I grabbed a few pillow cases and a few garbage bags and began packing Monique's clothes, Pampers and supplies, and a few clothing items for me, my work laptop, shoes, and my passport and other identification documents. I had no idea where I was going, but I knew I had to leave. Would I go back to New York? I decided against going back to New York because he knew where all my family members lived, and I did not want to put them at risk for what he threatened to do to me.

As I scurried down the stairs of the apartment complex to place some of the bags in the car, I caught sight of my ex-husband's car parked a short distance away. He was sitting in his car watching me. I quickly threw the bags in the car and hurried around the car to the driver's side. Before I could drive away, his car was facing mine blocking me from driving forward. While I was not skilled at reverse driving at the time, that was my only option to attempt a getaway where I was able to spin the car around at some point and drive forward in an attempt to exit the apartment complex. Looking back, it was like a getaway scene in an action-packed movie. He, however, took another direction and cornered me right before I was able to make the last turn on the main road out of the apartment complex, and using his car pushed my car with me in it backwards over 800 yards into a parking spot where I was now trapped by the apartment building behind me, a tree on my left, another car to my right, and his car directly in front of mine. Once I was cornered, he came out of his car with a car club (steering wheel device used to prevent car theft, remember we at one point lived in New York) and began smashing it against my driver's window, breaking off the side mirrors to my car. As he continued to hit the window with the car club, a few of Dekalb's finest arrived on the scene, sirens wailing loudly. I was relieved. My neighbors had witnessed the ordeal and called the police. He was arrested. A restraining order was issued. This was my opportunity to leave. Enough was enough.

I often think back to that day not because I wanted to keep the chain of events fresh in my mind but instead to think back to the marvel of God when He showed up for me in that moment.

While I did not notice it during the ordeal, God would show me later an image of His hands pressed on the inside of the window as my ex was hitting it with the car club in an attempt to break it.

Let's be clear though, I did not leave my ex-husband that day because I suddenly found my self-worth. I left as a means of survival. I had to survive for my daughter. Failure to understand my self-worth, my value, my identity kept me stagnant in a toxic relationship that had long run its course. When I made the decision to leave, I had no idea what the outcome would be. I was just tired of feeling broken and ashamed. It took years to unwrap myself from that marriage. Between the custody hearings, protective order hearings, divorce proceedings, and the continued threats from him, I was mentally and emotionally drained and broke.

We all have the power within us to break free from the toxic cycles that keeps us bound. I left that relationship with hopes that there were better days ahead despite still not appreciating the full essence of who I was. The vision and image of God's hands against that car window was enough to keep me moving forward—visualizing it gave me fuel to keep going. I knew at that point that in the midst of the chaos, He was present, allowing me to experience enough to wake up and know that it was time to move on from that toxic relationship but all the while protecting me from the devastation that could have been.

Where He guides, He Provides

In the midst of this valley, I learned that God is forever faithful and that He will never forsake me. I was new in my faith walk, being newly baptized two months prior to that final domestic attack against me. After my ex was arrested, I bounced from hotel to hotel for a few days. When that cost became too expensive, I called a coworker who ironically was the aunt of my brother's ex-girlfriend. She arranged for me to stay at her niece's house, where I stayed for a few days before leasing a new apartment. I struggled with moving out of state, but a speeding ticket kept me local. I received this speeding ticket the day after my ex-husband was arrested for pushing my car with me in it. I was on my way back from physical therapy (remnants of a car accident I'd had a few months prior) and was in a rush to get Monique from the sitter with the intent of leaving town before my ex-husband posted bail. This speeding ticket had a scheduled court date for two months down the road, and as a result kept me local.

For a long time, I was petrified of going out or being out after dark in fear that my ex would find me, and even after he found me the last time, that he would follow and harm me. I also struggled financially for some time. Between the legal fees, daycare expenses for my baby, student loan debt, credit card debt, a car note, and paying three rental lease payments (one lease payment for the current apartment I lived in at the time and two other partial lease payments for apartments I lived in previously and for which I broke the lease and moved each time my ex-husband found out where I resided). Not to mention that my ex-husband emptied our joint bank account (I did not have an individual account at the time) so there was no financial cushion for me and my daughter's needs. And to make matters worse, my ex-husband refused to pay child support, and refused to pay until eleven years later when he was forced to. But during this time my daughter and I were never hungry. I had no idea how I was going to survive when I left my ex, but as it says in Philipians 4:19, "my God will meet all your needs according to the riches of his glory in Christ Jesus." (NIV) God always provided.

Once our daughter became a little older, not only did she start asking questions about her father, but she demonstrated signs of trauma from the domestic abuse I endured and that she witnessed over the years. The first time I noticed this trauma displayed was during a visit to her paternal uncle's house. Her uncle and a couple friends were having a heated political conversation where at points their voices were extremely elevated. Baby girl was in her uncle's arms at the time and began trembling in fear not of him, but instead I believe she was fearful because the elevated voices to her meant danger was looming. She learned this because she had witnessed it so frequently. She lowered her head and used her two palms to profusely slap both her ears. It was enough to halt the conversation in the room. Her uncle then commented, "My brother has no idea how he damaged this baby girl."

Monique loved to read. A couple years after my divorce was finalized, I was in search of children's books that I could read to my baby girl to help her maneuver through her trauma and help her with some of her questions regarding her father's whereabouts. However, my search came up short as I mostly saw books geared toward same sex parenting households, or books focused on coping with divorced parents. That is until the day my Divine whispered into my spirit what I thought was a bombshell at the time.

I remember it like it was yesterday. I was standing in the middle of my 800 square feet one-bedroom apartment when I heard His voice: *"You cannot find it because I need you to write it."* Say what now! My response was, "You have the wrong daughter." A one-way conversation ensued that went like this: "First of all, where am I supposed to find the funds to fund such a project? Do you see my current mountains of debt?" But that was not the real issue. The real issue was I was operating from a place of fear. My greatest fear was that writing this children's book would expose me and my poor choices to the world. I pleaded, "Can you please give this task to someone else?" But He never responded to my rant. I had no choice but to start. I started with no idea what the first step was, or how I was going to pay for it. I started in fear and with an ounce of faith.

A few years later, not only was the book "I Forgive You Daddy; I Love You Anyway" written and published, but God also blessed me with a new home. God not only provided the means to accomplish that which He commanded me to do, but He also provided the means to release most of my debt (student loans still remained) and save enough to put a down payment and purchase my first home—a four-bedroom, three-bathroom, 3,376 square feet home a few months before the 2008 economic recession. I lived in that home with my baby girl for four years before I met my current husband and five years before I remarried. His provision went beyond finances as He also strategically placed the people I needed in my life and displaced the people around me that were an hindrance in an effort to elevate me to the next level and accomplish that which He entrusted me to do.

Love is patient, Love is kind

"Love is patient, love is kind. It does not envy, it does not boast, it is not proud. It does not dishonor others, it is not self-seeking, it is not easily angered, it keeps no record of wrongs." (1 Corinthians 13, NIV). While it is not always easy to tell at the beginning of a relationship if it will become abusive, it is important that one is able to recognize the signs, all of which are an effort to exert power and control over the abused (I have included a few of the signs at the end of this chapter). Of equal importance is understanding and appreciating the definition of love so that you can call a thing that which it is or is not when you are confronted with it. But oftentimes our own misunderstanding of who we are and the greatness for which we were created keeps us stagnant in toxic situations for way too long.

The road map to loving myself and to true success as I define it for myself included several wrong turns (and wrong relationships), many stagnant moments, and countless obstacles which unfortunately left me wounded for long moments in time. My experience with domestic violence was one of them. While this experience was devastating and could have been fatal, it was through this experience that my faith in and relationship with God grew stronger. I had to learn to trust that God would provide and protect me, just like He did in the car that day and countless other moments when I did not recognize it. It was through this experience that I learned to grow through the pain and love me as I was at that moment. It was through this experience that I learned what true love from a partner was not, so I could recognize what true love is when it showed up. It was through this experience that I began to envision what I wanted in my ideal future relationship so that when it showed up I could embrace it. It was through this experience that I learned that my words and my actions should always illustrate and encompass love because I learned first hand what it does to someone when one's actions and words doesn't. I pray that if you are reading this and are in or at some point find yourself in an abusive relationship, that you find God's hand to lead you safely out of it because He can, and you are so worth it.

Pause † Reflect

- Your mindset matters. You can only have the life that you believe you are worth.

- Your experience with domestic violence or any form of abuse does not decrease your value.

- You are worthy of relationships free of toxicity.

- You can overcome domestic violence. Overcoming starts with your first step out of the relationship and the environment.

- It is your responsibility to save yourself.

Signs of Toxic Relationships

(not an all-inclusive list)

Abuse occurs when one person in a relationship attempts to dominate and control the other person. Usually, the control begins with psychological or emotional abuse, then escalates to physical abuse. If you are seeing unhealthy signs in your relationship, it's important to not ignore them and understand that they can escalate to abuse. If you think you are in a dangerous situation, trust your gut and get help. If you or a loved one are a victim of domestic violence, contact the **National Domestic Violence Hotline at 1-800-799-7233** for confidential assistance from trained advocates. Below are some of the warning signs of a potential abusive partner, and are behaviors I experienced during my personal confrontation with domestic abuse by the hands of my daughter's father. Note that this list is not all-inclusive but instead are some of the common behaviors of toxic partners. Some partners may exert some or all of the behaviors.

🚩 **Extreme jealousy** - While jealousy is a normal human emotion, when it rises to the level where the person is trying to control what you do and who you spend your time with, it becomes unhealthy and is usually a sign that things are headed into toxic territory.

🚩 **Verbal abuse** - This can be evidenced in behaviors such as negative unconstructive criticism such as negative name-calling or other belittling comments targeted for degradation from your partner.

🚩 **Isolation** - An attempt by your partner to isolate you away from family, friends or other people. Similar to extreme jealousy it is usually a sign that things are headed into toxic territory. This usually occurs over a period of time and is oftentimes very subtle.

🚩 **Controlling behavior** - Attempts by your partner to control your actions or decisions or try to control what you wear, your appearance, where you go or who you talk to. This behavior is often difficult to identify or can be mistaken for love or genuine concern because it can be expressed in subtle or passive-aggressive ways.

🚩 **Projection of blame** - If your partner has a habit of avoiding personal responsibility for unhealthy behavior, or consistently views self as "victim" instead of "abuser/antagonist," or repeatedly making excuses for their bad behavior.

🚩 **Volatile mood swings** - Hypersensitivity and/or extreme unpredictable reactions from your partner that results in emotions of fear and confusion for the offended party. The slightest set back or response is perceived as a personal attack and as a result he/she usually lashes out verbally or physically.

🚩 **Acts of force/threats of violence** - This may involve actions from an abusive partner such as physical restraints, hitting, pushing, or shoving or the use of objects to manipulate you into doing what they want you to do or not do.

🚩 **Economic abuse** - The act of restricting your access to funds.

🚩 **Sabotage** - A purposeful attempt by your abuser to ruin your reputation with family, friends, coworkers, etc. in an attempt to negatively influence your relationship with others, impact your progress or your goals. This is usually a tactic aimed at isolation.

PART II

PART II

Disruption

"Only in the darkness can you see the stars."

Dr. Martin Luther King, Jr.

PART II

Disruption

> "Not all storms come to disrupt your life,
> some come to clear your path."
>
> *Gail Lee Gardner*

Disruption is oftentimes a process as opposed to an event. Within the narrative of our personal lives, and most definitely within my life as detailed within the context of this book, disruption is the process of redirecting our lives in a meaningful way—a realignment if you will. God will disrupt your entire being in an effort to heal you and unleash the greater purpose for which you were created. Disruption involves humility, breaking you down to your core just so He can pour new foundational elements in you to rebuild the foundations of your mind, brick by brick. Disruption is messy. Imagine renovating an old kitchen (hahem, I love interior design). Before you can install new cabinets, and accessories, you first have to demolish the old. The demolition is inevitably a messy process. Sure, you can paint the old cabinets and lay new tiles over the old, but this would be considered a facelift. Although a facelift tends to be less messy than an outright demolition, there could be foundational issues that are being ignored and that only a full-on demolition can uncover. If you try to fix a problem on the surface you will always come up short

God disrupted my life because its foundation had cracks in it and needed to be rebuilt; instability that was not evident on the surface but that subconsciously influenced all aspects of my life. Disruption was God's invitation into my healing. Embracing my disruption(s) propelled me into embracing my wholesome authentic self.

Chapter Four

Things Are Never Falling Apart; They Are Falling Into Alignment

"In order for God to work through us,
He must first do a new work in us."

Marshawn Evans Daniels

A breaking often happens right before a major breakthrough. You must go through the breaking before the healing.

Approximately six years after my divorce was finalized, I met my current husband. He is the complete opposite of any other man I had ever met. Instead of isolation, he promoted unity. He promoted love, in his own unique way. He is not afraid to tell me things as they are as opposed to that which he thinks I want to hear. Not to mention he is fine! The threats of violence, jealousy or the volatile mood swings I experienced in my past relationship were nowhere present. But like every relationship where you have two different people with all their past experiences seeking to join together in partnership, there are obstacles to work through.

Breaking Point

My breaking point left me lying on the floor of my master bathroom, curled up in a fetal position, immersed in a puddle of tears. I am not sure for how long I lay there. I wanted to get up but for some reason I just could not gather the energy to move. I did not want my daughter to find me like this but just could not find the strength to rise. I felt like the world as I had known it was being pulled from beneath my feet. I was overwhelmed with thoughts of not being enough. In fact, I had been fighting what felt like depression for some time—each day I literally had to fight what felt like dark clouds from consuming my entire world. My lifestyle was a far cry from where I started and for that I was grateful. But nothing would satisfy the emptiness I felt. Not even my frequent shopping expeditions geared toward pacifying my pain. In the words of Lauren Hill, *"How you gonna win when you ain't right within?"* At that moment I wanted to actually end my life and in fact at that moment was thinking through the fatal options in an effort to find the option that would be less painful and quick. But God kept me through the night, awake and alive as He flooded my thoughts of memories of me giving birth to my daughter, how valuable I was to her and what ending my life would do to her. He reminded me of my plea to Him to allow me the opportunity to conceive a baby girl so I could show her the love I never received, and how He had in fact entrusted me with my request. Was I going to quit on her now? I don't think I had any tears left in me by 6 am the next morning when I finally found the strength to pick myself up off the bathroom floor, get dressed, and drive to my brother's house. I did not trust myself at that point and was afraid the suicidal thoughts would resurface, and so before thinking it through I went to my brother, who lived approximately fifteen minutes away. As I shared my experience from the previous night with him, and the triggering event that led me to the bathroom floor with thoughts of ending my life, he listened attentively and reassured me that it would all work out and that he would always be a support system for me.

It did not end there! For the next few weeks I went into isolation. I deactivated all my social media accounts, turned my cell phone off for most of the time, and did not call or accept calls from family or friends, with the exception of my baby girl. My phone would only stay on if my daughter was not home or in my presence, just in case there was an emergency. I was hurting and cried pretty much daily. Just when I thought I had no more tears to shed, memories of my life's journey, every abusive and unwanted touch, every negative word spoken into me spiraled me further and further into depression. This went on for weeks until my paternal sister and my ride or die Meggie traveled to Georgia from New York to find out what on earth was going on with me and to whip me back to sanity. I was broken. This breakdown was in the making for a long time, but I had ignored all the warning signs as I had a tendency to compartmentalize my thoughts and issues as a coping mechanism.

Brokenness is not perceived as lovely in and of itself, and it sure is not a terminology you use when you want to feel your best self. The word itself depicts an image of shattered glass, a snapped rope, a splintered mirror, things appearing in complete disarray. Most of us despise broken things, often viewing them as unworthy to keep. But I offer you another vantage point on brokenness—it is not a destination, instead view it as an opening to a new path, a new beginning. There must be an opening through which true change can enter. Brokenness does not mean you are unworthy. Brokenness does not mean you should be discarded. Brokenness is the opportunity for God who began a good work in you, to put the pieces He originally minted back together, with the opportunity to evolve into a stronger being. My almost 20 years tenure in public accounting and working in a teaming environment has allowed me the opportunity to meet many people from quite diverse cultures. I enjoy learning about different cultures because it allows me the opportunity to advance my perspective. There was one particular conversation I had with a team member Eileen (her American name), who was born and raised in Japan and migrated to the US to pursue her higher education, that I think is quite useful to place here. We were discussing her favorite hobbies back home in Japan and the topic of pottery making came up, a hobby she had learned from her grandmother. She referred to it as "Kintsugi—the art of molding broken pottery pieces back together with precious metals." She went on to say that the underlying premise is that "nothing is ever truly broken and that through this art form the broken vessel has the opportunity to be stronger, unique and even more beautiful by embracing and highlighting its imperfections." The Kintsugi technique, according to the Internet of Things (IOT), highlights the scars as a part of the new design by molding each broken piece back together with lacquer mixed with precious metals such as gold, silver or platinum…treating the breakage and repair as part of the history of the object, rather than something to disguise. This conversation with Eileen resonated with me; similar to these broken vessels, our brokenness allows the opportunity for us to be mended, evolving us into stronger, unique, resilient and even more beautiful beings.

Brokenness is God's tool to equip us for His purpose. It is through our brokenness that God has the opportunity to enter into our lives and perform His great works. Today I stand in amazement in what God has done and continues to do with my once broken pieces. The beauty lies in where our brokenness leads us once we journey through the storm. This storm, unlike any other that preceded it, served as the disruption of me as I once knew her. It was the moment I could no longer rely on the coping mechanisms I developed over the years to distract me from my life issues, all of which compounded over the years and was now at the point of implosion.

Triggering Event

I was six years into my second marriage. A couple days prior to my breakdown, my husband and I had a mind-blowing, heartbreaking argument in the middle of marriage counseling. I wanted healthy boundaries to be established regarding previous relationships. He did not share the same viewpoint, and as a result he said some very hurtful things that triggered my childhood wounds of not feeling worthy of protection. Wounds I truly had not taken the time up to that point in my life to dissect and heal. I thought it safer to bury them because it would hurt too much to face them; the stitches would hurt more than the now numb wound itself. It is important to note that while the argument with my husband was a triggering point, I have come to realize that the pain in our lives may look like it is coming from a specific place or a specific relationship, when in fact it is being redirected from another place that needs attention and healing. I am not making an excuse for what my husband did in this space, for it stands alone—it was enough to trigger divorce discussions, and we came pretty close. However, the ability to be triggered by his statements or to be triggered by anyone outside of myself, for that matter, and the resulting impact on me meant there was something within me that needed healing—my value pot. It required me to dig deep within with God's divine guidance, to get to that tension spot, and to the root of my pain. It required me letting go and allowing God to perform soul surgery. A surgery that required opening me up, dissecting, removing and restoring, and yes, the application of stitches to put me back together again.

It is ironic that most of the time what we need to heal us appears to hurt more than the wound itself. It brings me back to a time after I had given birth to my daughter. She was in a breech position at thirty-six weeks into my pregnancy and the doctors thought it safer to deliver her by a Caesarean section because it was safer than being born vaginally. After her birth, the delivery wound required stitches so it could heal. Just like any other surgery, your body needs time to heal afterward, a process that requires rest, and not performing any extraneous activities for the specified time instructed by the doctor. However, a few days after I departed the hospital, I was not diligent to the doctors' recommendations (I was not getting the physical and emotional help I needed from her father and my now ex-husband) and I tore a few of the stitches applied to my wound. Long story short, my wound required a second round of stitching which appeared to hurt more than the first set, not only because I was heavily medicated for the first procedure, but because I had already grown accustomed to the wound. Revisiting the wound hurt. I feared the stitches. They were painful. But the stitches were necessary for the healing process. It was through this surgical experience that I truly recognized my innate V.A.L.U.E— that there is power in my Voice and my Visions; that there is treasure in my Aspirations and my Life experiences; that my Uniqueness is God's personal stamp on me; and my Existence is on purpose for a purpose. It was through this experience that my perspectives shifted— that half pint me equates to a full cup.

The pains of my past were plaguing my present because I defined myself up to that point based on the negative experiences in my childhood and that had perpetuated my adulthood. It impacted how I showed up in my relationships including my relationship with self—I did not see my value and as a result I did not establish safe boundaries for myself, thus settling for less than acceptable behaviour from others. It showed up in my career—I did not appreciate the value I brought to the table and in fact would often shy away from promotions and projects that would put me in the spotlight because I was convinced I would fail and God knows I did not need any additional failures to add to the list. The triggering event with my husband resurrected the wounds. If I wanted to heal, it meant I had to acknowledge my condition—every single wound, every hurt, every self-doubt from my past. But I could not do it alone. I needed His strength and guidance, for *"greater is He that is in me than he that is in this world."* (1 John 4:4 KJV). Disruption did just that. Disruption was the opportunity for me to surrender to God, and through the process of surrendering allowed Him to course correct my life. It was the opportunity for God to intimately and holistically prune the interconnected parts of me. It was the opportunity for Him to enter into my brokenness to dissect and remove the impressions that were not a part of His original plan, to deconstruct my thought patterns and the tainted and negative perspectives I had of myself, to dismember the opinions of others I had wrongfully attached as truth. The trigger showed me the pathway to my wound. His work in me allowed me to propel into a stronger, wiser and more confident version of me. I tell you all about the redefined her in part III. The old me could no longer sustain the new me I was destined to become.

Forward Is a Pace

About a month after the triggering event, I was having dinner with my dear friend Ms. Audrey. She was my daughter's pre-K and kindergarten teacher. She is an older lady, and I had a lot of respect for her, so I confided in her about my then struggles. She recommended that I seek spiritual counseling at our church, *Victory World International*. I immediately made an appointment and a couple Saturday nights later following our conversation I met with a counselor after church service. The counselor I connected with recommended me to an offered program titled "Forward" that was held at church every Sunday morning. It was a series of four transformational classes aimed at moving each person forward in their daily walk of life with Christ, followed by a conference weekend held twice per year for all attendees who completed the four classes.

When I made the commitment to attend the Forward program, I had no idea what the outcome would be. But what I knew for sure was that I was tired of feeling broken, broken from all the childhood traumas, broken from my bad decisions, and broken from my failures. My commitment to the program was my faith step to strengthen my trust in God. My commitment was a decision to step forward into growth which ironically required some shedding of the stuff that was tainting my perspective of self. The objective of our humanity is to grow. Oftentimes we as women allow the ridicule from others, the betrayals we experience, the traumas, or merely others' opinions to define us. As a result we show up mediocre to who we were created to be. The first step forward required a decision. The disruption will happen with or without input on your part, but growth will require a decision, a decision to move, a decision to surrender. It is in the midst of recognizing our imperfection that growth becomes possible.

The classes, as it turned out, were pivotal to my healing process, revolutionizing my thoughts and my thought process. Through this experience, God used the pain from my past and present to align me on the divine path to my healing. But He first had to show me what was holding me back. The process was hard but enlightening. I had the opportunity to shift my perspective of my past traumas, in the end realizing I was being equipped for what I was called to do. It was in the midst of the disruption under fire that I was truly born again.

Season to Be Still

There is work in stillness. *Rise by all means necessary* was my mantra during my disruption. Accordingly, weekly therapy was an added supplement to my healing process once the Forward classes ended. In the fall of 2018, right after my Thursday morning therapy session, the unimaginable happened—I endured a transient ischemic attack referred to in short form as a TIA or mini-stroke. Apparently I was experiencing symptoms for some time but was too focused on family and work and chalked the symptoms up to just being tired. Before I left therapy that Thursday morning, my therapist expressed her concerns regarding my consistently jam-packed schedule, which often included working on weekends, and advised that I needed to identify areas where I could take a step back so I could allow for complete healing. Absolutely not! My daughter and husband need me. My engagement team at work and my clients needed me; this was no time to cut back. We had just wrapped up an IPO (initial public offering) for my client, and at the time I was extremely busy assisting with the implementation of internal controls, a huge undertaking and a great resume building opportunity. This was not the time to pull back. Furthermore, I have worked sporadically since the age of thirteen and more steadily from age fourteen to date, so I was not accustomed to pulling back. Obviously the universe thought otherwise because shortly after leaving my 7:45 am therapy session and arriving at work, my symptoms kicked into gear as I progressively felt the left side of my body go numb! I literally felt like I was having an out of body experience but just could not define it. Whatever was happening, I could not let it happen in front of my team. In an effort to get to the emergency room (yes, I drove—which I admit was a bad idea) I pulled into an urgent care. Once I made it through the doors of the urgent care, I was immediately wheeled into a room and hooked up to an EKG monitor. I could vaguely hear the nurses in the background call out my stats to the 911 operator—I could hear the ambulance and the fire truck in the near distance, but I am not sure which one showed up first. Shortly after I was escorted by the ambulance to the nearest emergency room, where I spent the next few days being stabilized and ensuring I could do basic life activities like swallow and walk before being discharged. Subsequent to my discharge from the hospital, I spent the next several months in physical therapy in an effort to regain the strength on the left side of my body. This was my moment to pause and focus on holistic healing. But sometimes when it rains it pours. This was not the end of my health challenges. Subsequent testing and follow-ups after the TIA event noted three large tumors, two of which had to be surgically removed. And, as if this was not enough, prior to this surgery during my annual mammogram, a small lump was discovered in one of my breasts. This discovery led to repeated mammograms and ultra-sounds every two months for a year and a half to monitor the growth of said lump. Thankfully, the lump was eventually diagnosed as benign. But the mammogram process (there has got to be another way) was not pleasant.

Strange enough, throughout these challenges I was not scared. I had an uncommon sense of calm. I had no choice but to fully surrender. My Divine cleared my calendar—every meeting, every single "to do," every single deadline was cleared. I was too busy being busy. As a woman who constantly thinks she can "boil the ocean," I was accustomed to being everything and wanting to fix everything for everybody. It was my season to be still. I had no choice but to be okay with that. I was still to heal. I was still to just be. I was still to just observe. I was still to just listen to His direction. It was in this moment of stillness that our new business venture was conceived. The year after my TIA episode, our first Caribbean restaurant was born. I will tell you all about it later in chapter eight.

The disruption was pivotal to my becoming. It is for you too. The disruption itself does not define you. The intent is to clear the path to your greatness, to your divine purpose, to redefine who you think you are and bring you into alignment with who God minted you to be. I encourage you to embrace the process. Functioning under the ashes of shame and in the crevices of bro-kenness can feel safe because it is the known factor and is much less riskier than the unknown. But change is rarely ever easy. In our lowest moments, the most rewarding thing we can do is tap into something greater than ourselves.

Pause † Reflect

- Oftentimes pain in our lives may look like it is coming from a specific place or a specific relationship, when in fact it is being redirected from another place that needs attention and healing.

- Deliverance from our wounds is possible.

- There is no short-cut fix to deliverance. It is usually a step by step and messy process. The further we have buried the traumatic experiences, the more that will be necessary to eradicate it.

- Disruption is pivotal to our becoming. Trauma can be used as a lever to our growth.

- Disruption is the opportunity for God to enter into our lives and perform His great works.

Chapter Five

Soul Surgery

"The only person I have ever lost and needed back was myself."

author unknown

One of my favorite gospel songs is by gospel singer Tasha Cobbs Leonard, titled, *"Put a Praise on it!"* I claimed it. It served as my anthem song during the lowest point of my life. When you hit the ground floor, there is no other direction to go but up, or you can simply decide to stay there. I chose to believe that there was something greater for which I was purposed. I decided to rise and move forward. Remember my mantra—*Rise by any means necessary.*

Moving Forward

Truth is the starting point to our journey forward. Soul surgery required some self-reckoning, surrender and quite simply owning my stuff. The first of the four part series of the Forward class I mentioned previously was titled "Hearing God" and included teachings focused on our ability to hear God, the most common ways he connects with us, and the common hindrances that often prevent us from hearing Him. Prior to the end of the first class, the minister prayed and provided moments of silence for us to connect with God. Initially I struggled to calm my thoughts. Of course, being on the brink of a divorce for the second time, my heart was heavy with the disconnections in my marriage. As I closed my eyes, head leaning forward and nestled in the palm of my hands, I prayed and asked God why my marriage was failing. After all, I believed it was Divine intervention that we met based on how we were brought together. The subsequent whisper into my spirit was clear, gentle yet commanding, direct but non-judgmental: *Why do you expect your husband to prioritize your desires when you have not prioritized Me in your daily walk?*" It was not the answer I expected or wanted to hear. It was like going to marital counseling to fix your husband but hearing instead that you are the problem. Talk about adding shame to shame! I was embarrassed that I had not lived my promise I made fourteen years prior during my physical baptism: my promise to seek Him first. His words that followed were more comforting and was the perfect example of experiencing His grace: *"I am the light that will lead you out of the darkness, you must seek Me in everything you do."* That was my confirmation that brighter days were ahead, as long as I stayed directly connected to Him. Not long after that, the class was dismissed, but I stayed in position, focused on my direct one-on-one connection with God in that moment, completely oblivious to what was going on around me. Up to that point in my life I had only heard God's voice a handful of times, and when I did I always yearned for more. When I opened my eyes, most of the attendees had cleared out of the chapel. I wept bitterly that Sunday morning because for a short time I felt ashamed for not putting God first in my daily walk as I had promised the day I initially received Him into my life. But His comforting grace imparted a surge of strength within me to get up and face the storm. I was humbled. That day I made another promise to Him that my focus from that point on would be to build an authentic relationship with Him and to continuously seek him in all aspects of my life.

The Sabotage Cycle

Sabotage according to Merriam-Webster is the act of "deliberately destroying, damaging or obstructing a thing." The second series of the Forward class was titled "The Sabotage Cycle" and was focused on breaking unhealthy cycles in an effort to achieve true freedom. In this series I learned the four stages of the sabotage cycle, which starts with what is called "the event," defined as our experiences or what we did not experience, followed by the lie or otherwise referred to as the meaning we assign to the event. Trauma, our cultural environment, labels pasted on us by those around us and that we grow to believe are examples of "the event." How we interpret these events manifests the thoughts that fuel our inner saboteur or our self-limiting beliefs, causing us to outwardly manifest the resulting feelings of shame, unworthiness, and anger that usually stem from the negative events we experience, and thus self-sabotaging our actions, our goals, our desires, and our dreams.

It was during The Sabotage Cycle series at Forward that God revealed to me that pivotal moment as a five-year-old little girl where my inner saboteur was born—I told you all about that event in chapter one. The fuel for the sabotage was the lie. If we believe lies long enough, they become the fabric or the core from which we operate. At this moment, it became clear to me how the lie I interpreted from my mother's absence and the remnants of her not giving me her antique brush and comb set subconsciously influenced every decision I made, every thought I had from that moment on about myself, and how I showed up in the world up to my point of disruption. I was hiding my light, and I did not know where to find the switch to turn it on. My light was buried beneath the piles of experiences that fueled my sense of unworthiness. In my moment of healing, God opened a window to my past where I vividly saw the five-year-old version of me sitting at the edge of the bed in my grandparents' guest room, telling myself I was not enough. In an instant, He eradicated that lie and replaced it with His definition and purpose for me. Through Him I gained a new identity. In an instant, He redefined me and branded me with a new name—*Iridescence.* I was His light purposed to go out into the world for a *"town built on a hill cannot be hidden."* (Matthew 5:14, NIV). I was purposed in essence to be a rainbow, reflecting signs of hope for others weathering the storm.

But transforming my mind would be a process. To make radical progress, God had to reveal to me how my inner saboteur had impacted my life up to the point of my disruption. The months that followed were filled with introspection and eradication of old thought patterns and the accompanying shame in exchange for something new.

It was heavy.

It was ugly.

It was painful.

I was in the process of open mind surgery as God rewired my mind and my thought processes. It required intention. It required precision. It required finesse. God sure did have my full attention.

Overcoming self-sabotage was one of the most rewarding experiences I have ever endured because on the other side of it I gained emotional freedom and a depth of joy I could not have possibly imagined. I found her. The internal war with myself had finally ended. Iridescence was the victor, for she was now able to step into the greatest and most authentic expression of herself.

Through the Bristles of the Makeup Brush He Spoke

Foundation as the name suggests is the base layer on which you build, and in the world of makeup, it is the base upon which one builds their desired makeup look. The intent is to create a uniform color to our complexion or in some cases to cover our flaws. I was born with a birthmark on the right side of my cheek—a lighter patch of skin that was obvious to the naked eye, and which would often be misconstrued by my schoolmates as some form of deformity, leading to constant questions and often-times ridicule during my childhood years. When I started wearing makeup, for a long time the focus was just on the foundation—which one provided full coverage to hide my flaws. It was not until I was thirty years old that I started to dive into the other topical makeup applications such as blushes and eyeshadows.

"We believe that your beauty experience should be beautiful in itself." This was the slogan for the Rolls-Royce of makeup brushes known as Artis. I had often heard rave reviews about the

"Artis" brand, as reviewers and YouTubers raved about the brush's superior finish to their makeup applications. Since dabbling in makeup was one of my favorite pastimes since my 30th birthday, I was naturally curious. But the corresponding price tag was a splurge. Nevertheless, prior to my major disruption, and on one of my shopping ventures to Nordstrom, I decided to purchase the brush and settled on the Elite 10 foundation brush. The brush was noted to have over 250,000 individual and artificial fibers which made it perfectly designed to evenly distribute any foundation no matter the form. But this many fibers packed together also meant that the brush was not so easy to clean. There was an accompanying Artis brand cleaning system which also came at a hefty price tag, and which I decided to pass on at the time and instead rely on my "old school" castille cleaning mixture that I used for all my other makeup brushes. However, while the castille cleaning system worked for all my other brushes, getting the Artis brush completely clean remained a challenge. A few months later on another shopping trip to Nordstrom during their anniversary sale, I was able to purchase the Artis foam cleaning system on sale. Guess what, it worked like a charm.

Months after my disruption and at the tail end of my healing (I was now back at work, part time but working nonetheless), on a rainy Sunday afternoon, I was cleaning my makeup brushes which was a frequent Sunday ritual. I continued to use the castille system on all my brushes with the exception of the Artis brush-at $17 for a 32 oz size bottle, it was quite cost efficient. I cleansed, rinse and laid all the other brushes out to dry before turning to the special cleansing routine I had for the Artis foundation brush. It required hot water, the Artis foam cleanser and a rigorous scrubbing process to eliminate all the foundation debris from the brush. That Sunday afternoon as I administered the final rinse to the brush, observing the now clear water running down the drain, which served as confirmation that the brush was now in fact clean, I felt His divine presence and heard His whisper "only the creator can wash you clean" within my spirit. I smiled as I reflected on His words, all present in the moment and what it represented. I felt like He literally took a brush and dusted me off at that moment. I felt comforted. I felt clean. I felt like I mattered. I felt like His Masterpiece. It resonated. I happily cried. There was no other cleaning system that worked on the Artis brush outside of the cleaning system created by the manufacturer specifically for their designed brushes. Similarly, only the Creator was able to truly renew my mind (and yours too) and my sense of identity, redefining me from the measures of the world to propel me into who He minted me (us) to be.

His Truth

God spoke to me the truth. He took me back into my story, into my wounds, and He helped me to renounce and counteract the lies I told myself and that others spoke over and into me. He strengthened me to forgive myself and others that inflicted pain on me or whose lack of protective actions caused me to doubt my worth. I realized through this process of disruption that my life no longer had to be defined by the story I'd journeyed thus far. The challenging times were a part of my journey and not the definition of who I am as a person. I was confident that I was in His capable hands. Disruption accentuated the parts of me that I needed to emerge into greatness.

Pause † Reflect

- It is important to understand that other people's opinions of you are not facts. Just because someone doesn't see your worth doesn't mean you are of no value.

- What once was a source of pain can be a source of strength for you and for others.

- You are worth fighting for. The key is to faithfully depend on Him to define and equip you with what you need to overcome.

- The biggest gap between where you are and where you want to be is tapping in to the authentic you.

- Growth will require you to release the baggage of your prior phase.

- When things change inside of you, things change around you.

PART III

PART III

The Redefinition of Her

"Do not conform yourselves to the standard and the patterns of this world, but let God transform you **INWARDLY** by a complete change of your **MIND.** Then you will be able to know the will of God what is good and is acceptable and what is indeed perfect."

Romans 12:2 GNB

PART III
The Redefinition of Her

"Shifting your mindset is the alchemy
to uncovering the authentic you."

Georgia Wolfe-Samuels

The biggest hurdle I have ever had to overcome in my life journey was eradicating faulty thinking about myself, and rewiring my mindset to *believe bigger*, recognizing that I am not by any means a limited edition but instead a unique edition empowered to dream and achieve great things. Guess what! We are all unique editions intentionally crafted for a special purpose, created to do good works. But recognizing and embracing this fact is dependent on our mindset and how we define ourselves. Shifting our mindset is the alchemy to uncovering the authentic you. The traumas, wounds, and pain we experienced in our lives deserves our full attention, dissection, resolution and ultimate healing. The purpose of disruption in my life was to kill the unauthentic version of me and redefine me in accordance with how God created me to be. That is the purpose of disruption! Redefining Her ... You, may look different for each of us, I give you snippets of my path in the next few chapters. However, Redefining you will require intentional actions and a commitment on your part to realign to God's definition of and desire for you. Here are some ground rules to redefining you:

R - Renew your mindset. Your mindset is the alchemy to uncovering the authentic you. Your thoughts create your reality – your happiness and success are interconnected to your mindset. Your mindset should mirror your aspirations. Ideate your desires and create a new mental script, reinforcing with actions that supports your aspirations.

E - Embrace all of who you are, flaws and all. Embracing who you are is the act of appreciating oneself and performing actions that support you, understanding that you are not perfect (no one is).

D - Debunk that which does not serve you. Do not give credit to the negative opinions of others, or labels and habits that does not represent the authentic you. Choose instead a new mental script that is in tune with who you genuinely are (it starts with your thoughts).

E - Environment. Evacuate environments that are harmful or that do not support your aspirations.

F – Forgiveness. Forgive yourself for past thoughts, actions and lack of actions. Forgive others for their transgressions. Forgiveness shifts your response to the memory going forward.

I – Invest in you. Invest in yourself by taking concrete action steps aimed at bringing you closer to your highest and most powerful self—you are worth it!

N - Nurture your value. Make yourself a priority, embracing activities that support you and allows you to feel more joyful, knowing at your core that you are worth it.

I - Imagine from a place of abundance, believing that you have all that you need within you.

N - New meaning. Apply new meaning to your triggers. Our wounds should inform us, not define us.

G – Grace. Gratitude. Growth. Extend grace to yourself and others. Practice gratitude, frequently. Commit to continuous growth.

H - High bar. Set a high bar for yourself, you are capable.

E - End of others. The end of others and the beginning of you- establish safe, healthy and sustainable boundaries.

R - Respect and trust the process. Respect and trust the process, and by all means remain in the vine, reciprocating all that which you desire.

The Redefined *Her* is:

Healed from all the debilitating mental constructs that weigh her down, Empowered for impact and Restored into her authentic self.

Transformation Guide©

REDEFINING HER©

VISIONS

GOALS

CAREER

MENTAL HEALTH

ENTREPRENEURSHIP

WEALTH

PHYSICAL HEALTH

RELATIONSHIPS

CONFIDENCE

Renew your mindset.
Embrace all of who you are.
Debunk that which does not serve you.
Evacuate environments that are harmful.
Forgive yourself and others.
Invest in you.
Nurture your value.
Imagine from a place of abundance.
New meaning to our triggers.
Grace. Gratitude. Growth

High bar. Set a high bar for yourself, you are
capable.
End of others. Establish safe , healthy and
sustainable boundaries.
Respect the process.

HER

Mindset Shift

Chapter Six

Embracing Her

> "I can't go back to yesterday because
> I was a different person then."
> *Alice in Wonderland by Lewis Carroll*

You are the only you that there will ever be, uniquely crafted by God, uniquely purposed for His will, a unique edition. May you embrace your true identity so that the missiles thrown by this fractured and harsh world never come close to piercing your authentic being, knowing at your core that you are worth it. As you discover who and Whose you really are, you will never want to go back to yesterday or be someone else again.

We all experience significant events in our lives that change and mold us in a fashion that makes who we were before we experienced them unrecognizable. The most impactful events impacting my identity to date have been described within this book. I can't even recall the chain of events or who I was prior to that defining moment with my mother at age five. What was I like before that incident? Was I full of courage? Was I adventurous? What were my thoughts about myself? However, ever since

I redefined myself through His lens, I "have put on [my] new self, which is [continuously] being renewed in knowledge in the image of [my] creator." (Colossians 3:10) NIV

During the disruption, God rebranded me "Iridescence." The name Iridescence encompasses a myriad of definitions: light, glowing, to illuminate, or a play of lustrous changing colors. As Iridescence, I am not just a reflection of different colors, I shine from within. I am multidimensional, in a complex way, possessing various talents, gifts, and interests. As His light, I don't just reflect light, I am light. Light allows for sight and visibility. Light stems from many sources—from a burning flame, from the sun, from the moon, from a light bulb powered by electricity, etcetera. The underlying commonality among these sources is power. My light was forged in the flames of my experiences giving me power for my purpose. Once I understood this, it became easier for me to fully embrace me and come to terms with the myriad of experiences along my journey, including the not so favorable ones. My experiences were exactly that: experiences. My experiences are not my identity, but instead they were the fires that forged and strengthened me for my purpose. From this vantage point, things began to change.

Trust in Thyself

"We can lose self-trust in many ways,
but one day you will realize you had it all along."

Georgia Wolfe-Samuels

Our true nature as human beings is to trust. We were born with a natural instinct to trust, trusting that when we cried, our needs would be tended to, whether we needed a diaper change, food, or simply to be cuddled. Oftentimes we begin to lose trust when the people that are closest to us hurt us, or when others in the world manipulate us for their own self-gain. These experiences in turn have a ripple effect, undermining our trust of self and ultimately our self-confidence. As I noted in Chapter 1, children are good receptors and very bad interpreters primarily because they lack the wisdom and experiences to assess situations and conversations for themselves. As a public accounting auditor and a certified public accountant by trade, I am trained to be skeptical. It is the foundation of the public accounting profession. Skepticism is used in the validation of information through methods such as the critical assessment of evidence and paying particular attention to inconsistencies in evidence obtained, some of which is obtained based on probing questions we are trained to ask our clients. Unfortunately, this skillset is not inherent in our nature as children and even in some adults. We do not question our caretakers—at least back in my day you dared not! Growing up in Jamaica, children were groomed to be seen and not heard. You dared not ask questions when you were told to do a thing, and you dared not backtalk when you were called a thing! As a result we journey through life believing who others told us we are—we don't ask the probing questions or assess the labels for evidence to determine for ourselves whether they are in fact true. Our journey to learning to trust ourselves again will require methods to eradicate all the mislabels and misinformation that were erroneously allowed to shape our identities and ultimately affect our day-to-day decisions, thus impacting how we flowed in the world. Our decisions and our actions in many ways determine the quality of our life experiences. When I trust in what I think and feel, I am emboldened to make decisions and take actions that support me. Once I started to trust and believe in myself, I began to experience life differently. But first I had to learn to forgive myself. I had to forgive myself for:

- Allowing myself to remain in an abusive relationship.

- For accepting and operating from the labels placed on me from others close to me.

- For shying away from job opportunities because I was afraid of rejection or not performing up to the expectation of others, and simply because I did not believe and trust in myself.

- For not following my intuition when a situation did not quite feel right.

- For being hard on myself when efforts to lose weight failed.

- For acting in ways that were counter to my true core values.

- For faulting myself when forgiving my father took longer than I expected, even after I became a Christian.

- For at times not establishing with others in my life the boundaries I deserved and needed.

Forgiving myself paved the way to allow room for self-trust. Self-trust fueled my confidence. I learned that if I did not trust myself, then I surely did not trust God, meaning I did not trust that He had created me in His liking for a specific purpose. Learning to trust myself took time and intention. When you meet someone that you have a spark of romantic interest in, you are intentional in spending time to date that person (in some cases) to learn their interests, likes and dislikes. While I did not have a romantic interest in myself, I had a vested interest in showing up from a place of wholeness. I began spending intentional alone time with myself assessing my likes, my dislikes, my traits (both negative and positive), what sparks my interests, what are my emotional triggers, all in an effort to truly get in tune with myself so I could fully embrace her.

During my recovery period, I took my first bold step on my new life venture to discovering me and booked a solo trip to San Francisco for a weekend to attend the "Know Your Value" conference, allotting myself some time to explore the city (ahem … shopping). My family was a bit fearful of me taking this trip especially by myself since I was still in recovery. It was an invest-ment in me. It was my first time ever visiting the West Coast and my first time traveling solo for a non-work related trip. I took an early flight from Atlanta, arriving at my hotel in downtown San Francisco around noon West Coast time. Since check-in was not until 3 pm, I left my baggage with the hotel concierge and ventured off to explore the city, stopping first at The Rotunda at Neiman Marcus for lunch. I opted for a table as opposed to sitting at the bar where it wouldn't be obvious that I was dining alone. I did not care about the optics—a table for one please. Yes, there were a lot of cheaper alternatives for lunch, but I decided on The Rotunda and I was okay with that—in that moment and from thence forth I embraced that I have an appetite for elegance and I was unapologetically okay with that fact. I savored my two-course lunch starting with a lobster bisque soup for appetizer followed by a pan-seared salmon for my main course, with a glass of white wine amid the stares of the other guests. I was so focused on myself and just being in the moment that it was not until I asked for the check that I noticed I was the only black person in the restaurant, the only solo diner at a table, and the only person casually dressed. After all, it was a weekday. I was not fazed. After lunch I ventured off for a mini shopping spree (my carry-on could only fit so much) treating both myself and my mini me to a couple unique pieces and gathering a couple items for my husband's upcoming birthday. As I strolled through the stores searching the racks, a sense of peace engulfed me—it felt good that my purpose for shopping had changed. I was no longer shopping as a means to mask my pain, I was shopping because it is good cardio (this is proven), and I quite frankly like to do it.

I walked the city for the remainder of the afternoon into the early evening taking in the culture of the city, most of which was rather depressing due to the high rate of homelessness and as a result the plethora of homeless people sleeping on the streets, in addition to the crowds of protesters rallying against unfair labor practices. I stopped at a park and sat on a side bench, observing my surroundings and taking a moment to not just be in the moment but to also reflect on my own experiences with homelessness as a teenager (and again after I left my first husband) and how my paternal sister and I were able to overcome these challenging times. In that moment I was feeling extremely thankful to God for carrying us through to the point where both my sister and I now owned the homes we live in and are both educated and blessed with rewarding careers that allow us the ability to provide for our families, including our aging father. What would our lives be like had we not relentlessly kept moving, even when the path was not clear? Although I did not define it as such at the time, our actions during these challenging times working full-time hours while attending high school and thereafter our respective colleges to ensure we could pay our overhead expenses and take care of ourselves, sacrificing teenage pleasures were in fact an indication of trust. Though we were in fact subconsciously trusting ourselves and the universe as we went through the day-to-day motions, trusting that our hard work would one day pay off, back then we just titled it survival. It was apparent that self-trust was a key ingredient for us to keep propelling forward to our goals. Another character trait became clear. In that moment while sitting on the park bench in downtown San Francisco, I embraced another characteristic—resilience. It was also quite clear that trust of self was there all along and just like our muscles just needed to be acknowledged and exercised more frequently.

Know Your Value

"If you don't know your value and you can't communicate
it effectively, you're leaving money on the table—
not just at work but in any relationship."

Mika Brzezinski

You are a masterpiece! You were uniquely crafted, custom-made with different gifts, talents, dreams, perspectives, visions, and identities, on purpose, with intention by a God of purpose. The moment you embrace this fact, is the first step in the healing process and the healed soul will begin to recognize its intrinsic value—an intangible that no money in this world can buy.

Knowing your value is knowing yourself. Knowing your value will require a better understanding of your unique strengths, weaknesses, tendencies, and emotional triggers, all with a target goal to show up from a place of wholeness in your day-to-day relationships, in your workplace, in your businesses, and most importantly for yourselves. Knowing your value is not finite. It is a continuous journey, discovering and embracing more of you each and every day. The greatest takeaway for me from the Know Your Value Conference in San Francisco was embracing the fact that I can do anything once I believe I can. Before attending the conference, as far as I could recall, I had a tendency to shy away from any opportunity that required me to speak to a group of people, especially on camera—*no thank you!* This is contrary to stories told by my father and other family members who often noted that as a toddler I could not hold water and would speak to anyone that would listen. But somewhere along the way, that little girl was muted (ahem, the experience with my mother I told you about in chapter 1). For the conference, I decided to wear a bright red long sleeve DVF sheath dress, selected as the dress of choice by my husband. Red was not my usual color choice as it would garner too much attention. Just in case I changed my mind, I also packed a plain white dress and a black dress. As I entered the conference registration area next to the ballroom where the conference was being held, I was approached by a cameraman who I would find out later worked for NBC. *"I will come find you later for an interview, you can't hide in that dress,"* he stated with a smile before disappearing into the crowd. Great! Somehow I have to figure out how to blend in with the hundreds of women and very few men at the conference, and that is exactly what I attempted to do until I heard the voice I feared over my shoulder during our lunch break.

"Are you ready for your interview?" he asked and before I could answer he began going over the protocols of the interview. *"I just need five minutes of your time to talk about a know your value moment in your life."* As he continued to speak, I mustered up the energy to tell myself, *"Girl, you can do this,"* and I actually believed in that brief moment that I could. At the end of the interview, the interviewer commented, *"Girl, you were radiant, you were made for this."*

That feedback gave me a confidence boost. I felt extremely proud of myself. God used that moment to show me that my (and yours too) most valuable resource is our mind, and whatever we believe we can do we can actually do it. In order to be my best self I (and you too) have to take care of our minds. The conference experience brought other valuable nuggets, including the importance of using my voice, of finding the courage to take the unpopular paths, and to be authentically me as opposed to acting like it.

When you know your value, you show up differently.

I Am (You Are) More Than Enough

I am more than enough! Scream it from the mountain top or the valley low, I am more than enough! Embracing me (you) is not a physical act like a hug, but instead is the mindset of removing the negative self-judgment when we make mistakes, when our relationships fail, or even when the opportunities we seek do not materialize. I am more than enough does not mean

I (you) have reached the pinnacle of our achievements, growth or learning but instead symbolizes that we are in full acceptance of ourselves as we are today. I am more than enough means that I (you) don't have to be everything and all things. I (you) am more than enough does not thrive on self-sufficiency but instead means that we are in tune and in full acceptance of who we are, our strengths, our weaknesses, and knowing that our flaws do not reflect our value, and through it all we are worthy.

Combatting the deeply rooted build-up of internalized negative messages, whether they were internally crafted from our own traumatic experiences or inflicted on us by others can be quite a task. We must embrace and love ourselves exactly as we are today, not waiting for who we will be tomorrow after we have achieved a certain metric on the scale, or when we finally graduate, or when we get that new job or new position, or that holy hookup. It is okay for wanting to make certain adjustments and setting goals for further advancements, but we must love and embrace ourselves in the process because we are more than enough. Embracing who we are today does not mean we are settling for a lower version of who we are but instead accepting and trusting that we are more than enough as handcrafted by Christ, we are Christ's handiwork. We are more than enough means that we are whole, fully equipped

to be,

and to seek,

and to dream,

and to achieve,

and to step into our greatest self.

Pause † Reflect

- Regardless of your past trauma, your weight, body proportions, flaws or mistakes, you are more than enough.
- Believing in yourself and changing your life trajectory takes courage.
- Believing in yourself takes bravery.
- Believing in yourself will require grace and forgiveness.
- Believe in yourself because you are worth it.

Chapter Seven

Healing Her

"Be like a tree and let the dead leaves fall."

Rumi

The Girl in the Mirror

My personal healing started with the girl in the mirror because true change begins with self. Embracing me in my then current state. Forgiving me for the disobedience, the indecisions, the bad decisions, and the decisions I initially thought were good decisions. My first step was to work on rebuilding my relationship with God in a truly authentic way. To uphold the promise I made to seek him daily. The opportunity to attend the Forward series during my disruption opened up new desires for God as He step by step replaced my trauma, the hurt, the pain, and the negative self-perception with more of Him. To set the stage for each day, I committed my first moments of every day to connecting with Him through devotion, prayer, or simply just having a conversation with Him. These moments are not timed in an effort to release any constraints. In transparency, there were days when my efforts felt a bit rushed but over time and allowing some small tweaks (i.e. getting up earlier) it became effortless. My experience in these moments were manna for my day, setting the stage for how I showed up. I openly submitted to Him and allowed Him to guide my thoughts.

Note that God created within all of us the human brain which produces our every thought, action, memory, and feeling. While I am by far not a neurologist, when I think of the brain in relation to the mind, I use the analogy of a fruit bearing tree where the brain is the root, the mind is the tree trunk from which springs branches, otherwise known as our thoughts, which then bear fruits. The productivity or positivity of those thoughts determines the fruits that tree bears, if any. He gave us the choice to think thoughts. Please know that I am in no way discrediting or minimizing the powerful resources found in medicine or counseling for I too have used the latter (as I have openly discussed within), and I truly believe that there are seasons where these resources may be necessary. What I am saying is that in each and every second of each and every day we have access and the power to change our trajectory through Him and by being intentional in our thoughts. The goal is not to prevent all negative thoughts because that is not practical. The goal is to manage our response to our negative thoughts.

Knowledge will save you. Becoming spiritually centered also included fellowship at my home church, Victory World International, which was in person for the most part until the COVID-19 pandemic forced us all online, seeking books from authors like Iyanla Vanzant, Brene Brown, and Marshawn Evans-Daniels that were focused on spiritual growth, personal growth and dreaming bigger, watching YouTube sermons from Bishop TD Jakes, Pastor Robert Madu, and Joyce Meyers, just to name a few. My morning and evening rush hours to and from work (prior to the COVID-19 pandemic) were the opportune moments to lean in and receive His word. Through these mediums I learned how to tune into the meaning of my experiences, looking beyond and deriving meaning from what I can't necessarily see with my naked eyes.

Gratitude will humble you. Gratitude also opens the door for abundance thinking -believing that what is for you will be for you and there is enough room in this world for you to shine in your own time. I calibrate my day daily beginning with a read of whatever devotional I have in my arson, some of which are physical books or an app such as YouVersion. I journal daily which allows me to embrace and amplify my daily blessings and helps me to counteract thoughts of not being or having enough.

What We Tell Our Mind, We Become

"Be transformed by the renewing of your mind."

Romans 12:2

Change your thoughts, change your world. Our thoughts influence our emotions and our attitudes, which fuels our habits, which creates our reality. We all experience in our lives what I call knee moments. These are moments when situationships or experiences do not allow us to experience the victory we seek, oftentimes bringing us to our knees in moments of perceived weakness, coloring the lens through which we view ourselves and the experience itself. God met me on my knees in the midst of overwhelming hurt and shame and spoke to me His truth.

He renounced the lies I told myself and the ones told to me by others, including others tasked with caring for me, and replaced them with His truth. But I had a responsibility for my own healing too. I had to take control of my thoughts. Continuous healing required me to change how I spoke to myself, even in moments when I am not victorious. Changing my language required changing my thoughts. Changing my thoughts required changing my mindset, which required daily reminders, popularly known as affirmations that would counteract any negative thought and support me in my growth. Affirmations served as an empowering tool that helped me learn how to select and curate my thoughts similarly to how I am selective in what I wear every day. Just as eating is a daily practice, so is loving ourselves. Our self-talk fuels our reality and over time will rewire our brain and ultimately our thoughts and habits, bringing us the true peace and joy we desire. Some of my profound growth came from not just speaking affirmatively to myself, but journaling my thoughts real time, documenting the feeling a particular affirmation or experience aroused within me. A few of my daily affirmations are below, some of which were handwritten in my "Mac ruby woo" lipstick across my bathroom mirror as I transitioned through my disruption:

- I am healed
- I am whole
- I am in charge of me
- I am enough in my becoming
- I am beautiful, inside and out
- I am love and I am worthy of love
- I am well-able to do that which He has planted in me

- I am stepping into my power, one day at a time
- My thoughts and opinions matter

Emotional Triggers

Emotional triggers are those painful emotions that are triggered by experiences that are reminiscent of old painful feelings. It can be daunting to identify what exactly our emotional triggers are, but the process of getting to know and understand them can help us heal and learn coping mechanisms for better responses that truly serves us. The ability to feel different emotions is one of the most painfully enlightening privileges we have. In a moment of transparency, there were times in my current marriage when my husband and I would have an unresolved disagreement, and he would isolate himself in a separate room for days, appearing perfectly fine as he went about his daily routines. While this may have served as a coping mechanism for him and a means to ease the tension between us, for me it would continue to infect the wound or fuel the fire to our disagreement. For years this act would irritate me, and I would interpret his actions as a lack of care and respect, triggering further a response from me that was dishonoring to my core and to our marriage. In actuality, his action simply reminded me of my abandonment issues with my mother and at some point my earthly father as well. Moments where I felt abandoned, unvalued or unheard served as emotional triggers. Knowing the origin of our triggers is the first step to managing them because it is imperative that we are proactive in creating a strategy to resolve and prevent us from being enslaved to it/them. With the help of my therapist, I learned to identify and acknowledge my triggers without giving them permission to control my thoughts and ultimately my actions. The next step involved ensuring when triggered that I was present in the moment, thus disabling my thoughts from wandering to my past experiences while allowing me to determine if the threat was in fact real and worthy of a response because not all feelings are facts. This is a continuous journey, the goal of which is to act and respond from a place of **POWER** (Perspectives. Optimism. Wisdom. Empathy. Respect), and in a manner that honors my core and the future I aspire, knowing that my triggers serve to inform me as opposed to defining me.

Mastering Me

It is truly amazing what we can do when we realize we have the power to change our own lives. What better way to put my newfound confidence in development to the test than to seek challenging experiences. Healing required challenging myself to do the hard things during the healing process. I challenged myself to take on the hard tasks in my professional career and found myself speaking up in meetings without being paralyzed by fear as I had grown accustomed, despite at times being the only female and most times the only black person in the room. Each success boosted my confidence more. I also stepped up in my personal life as well, saying yes only when I had the capacity to fulfill the request. I intentionally tried to be present in the moment most of the time (versus constantly thinking about the next thing on my task list or checking off the mental checklist). I began crafting my vision for my life (of course allowing God into the details). I was thoughtful and deliberate in how I wanted to make others I encountered feel, how I wanted to dress, personal aspirations, family goals, my career goals, and entrepreneurship goals. For the first time in my life I was not afraid to dream bigger. I did it scared. I made a commitment to growth and empowerment both internally and externally and made a promise to continuously invest in me.

Pause † Reflect

- You are where you are on your journey, and that is beautiful and it is enough. Give yourself grace.
- Your failure and mistakes were an event, not a personal characteristic.
- Growth is a direction, not a destination, forever becoming.
- There is no shortcut. It takes time to rebuild the true version of you. Be patient with yourself.
- Set your standards—self-care, soul-care and healing work must become a non-negotiable.

Chapter Eight

Her Redefined

"The foundational base of Redefining Her is rooted in what She believes about Her core self. The first step in Redefining Her is knowing at Her core that she is worth it."

Georgia Wolfe-Samuels

Ident?ty Redefined
I am Worthy. I am Purposed.
I am more than enough.

"Anyone who has discovered who God has made them to be would never want to be anyone else."

Bill Johnson

As women, we are often defined by the roles we play in life, what society defines as acceptable or unacceptable for us, or by some other attributes such as our physical traits, the color of our skin, etcetera. We have historically had to fight for our equality and if you ask me, the fight still continues. Women had to fight to own property. Women had to fight for the right to vote. In some countries women are still not allowed the privilege of an education. The world continuously screams at us, telling us we are not enough. On the eve of publishing this memoir, the first ever woman, and first african american, M.V.P. Kamala Harris, was elected to be the Vice President of the United States of America. I never thought in my wildest dreams I would live to witness this becoming. It was a powerful and inspirational experience. But her journey to the second highest position was met with great ridicule, as some critiqued her qualifications based on the fact that she is a woman, and especially a daughter of immigrants, and therefore was viewed as not strong enough in the event the President died during his term and she had to take the reigns. Her career history was scrubbed and scrutinized, and rightfully so, but this all seemed unimportant to the majority during the elections of past vice presidents. We still have a long way to go but Kamala has paved the way for us to dream bigger, and know that we too can.

How we show up is directly impacted by how we see ourselves, which is often affected by our life experiences and the different ways we allow the world to define us. I told you bits of my story. Oftentimes I hear women question their worth, unsure of the meaning of their lives. As I have told you within this book, for the majority of my life I did too. While it is perfectly natural to ponder the value in our existence, the issue arises when we look outside of ourselves to define ourselves. Discovering my identity according to how God defines me was and remains the greatest achievement in my life. Knowing and understanding my identity in Christ required a new mindset—a renewing of my mind. I had to *put on [my] new self which is being renewed in knowledge in the image of its Creator (Colossians 3:10 NIV)*. How God defined me had no connection to my career, who my parents are, who my friends are, the color of my skin or my past failures. Be clear on who you are, for when we don't know who we are, we are in fact saying we do not know who God is. On the other side of disruption, I discovered me, the core component of who I am. I dare you to be vulnerable and trusting enough to believe in yourself. The journey will not be easy but it is the disruptive moments that reveals our truth and on the otherside elevate us way beyond our wildest imaginations.

Self-definition has proven to be one of the highest hurdles I had to jump. Similar to peeling back the layers to determine the fuel to my inner saboteur, I had to peel back the layers of my personality and determine what intricate parts I wanted to define how I showed up. Only powerful and uplifting terminologies are allowed as part of my lexicon, so that I am fully armed when instances of doubt creep in (because in reality they will). I remind myself of these words daily.

I am Resilient because I survived 100 percent of the obstacles I encountered and am well equipped to overcome the obstacles yet to come.

I am Bold because in the presence of fear I armor and go forth with the Holy Spirit.

I am Iridescence, God's light qualified by my journey, armored with my story and purposed to bring light to other Queens and to the world.

I sought to understand these truths and align myself accordingly. Aligning myself meant I had to make a conscious effort to direct my thoughts. I had a renewed focus on these truths. Once I believed these truths, I started to show up differently, knowing that when hardships present themselves (because they will), I have what it takes within me to overcome. I have had tremendous success with my shift in mindset approach; I became confident in my walk with God, and as a result I began to raise my hand for new and challenging opportunities in my professional career. My renewed confidence also allowed me to boldly leverage my passions and creative skill sets, which included interior design and strategies for business design and growth into the creation and opening of our first Caribbean Restaurant. The revelation of my light provided the insight to write this memoir with the intention of leveraging my story to motivate other women to dispel the lies of their inner saboteur and to provide guide rails on how to overcome them. I am no longer defined by my story, but instead, my story qualified me to do God's work. My story qualified me to stand confidently. Redefining her (me) means I have new standards to live by. Redefining her (me) means I think differently. Redefining her (me) means I act differently in reflection of who she (me) is authentically, looking nowhere but within myself for the motivation to see the world from a different perspective and to garner the courage to unveil my gifts and talents to progress forward. You too have talents and gifts—I believe our unique purpose is to use our talents and gifts to ignite progression in this world and to make a difference for humanity. But if your mindset does not allow you to boldly utilize your gifts and talents, then the world will not experience your impact.

Our mindset is the key to us showing up like champions, empowered for impact. But our mindset is based on the premise of a solid foundation, free of cracks, focused on our power and our future, not the mistakes of our past, or our potential failures. You cannot build an elevated framework on a foundation with cracks in it, it is unstable. Reflect on the guidance provided in what has grown to be my favorite scripture—II Timothy 1:7 "For God has not given us a spirit of fear, but of power, love and a sound mind" (NKJV). We already have all that we need within us.

Nurture My (Your) Value

If your starting point is a place of self-doubt, coming to the realization that you have value (and always had) may be quite a daunting task, requiring a lot of patience and intentional actions on your part to nurture and grow it, starting with our thoughts and the things we consume mentally, spiritually, and visually to nurture them. Know that we have within us the power to change the trajectory of our thoughts and ultimately our lives. To move beyond our status quo, we must recognize the connection and power of our thoughts and how they impact our habits and ultimately the quality of our lives and the manifestation of our dreams. Our value to us women (and men too) is like what soil is to a plant—an anchor, providing water and nutrients to allow for growth. Similarly, redefining her (you) is rooted in what you believe about yourself. Once you embrace your V.A.L.U.E. (Voice and visions. Aspirations. Life experiences. Uniqueness. Existence.), you will require continuous nurturing. Nurturing comes in various forms. For me it involves self-care (lots of it). My self-care routine ranges from spa days, skin care routines, massages, physical exercise, daily devotion, meditation, shopping (in moderation), rest time, etc. Nurturing me also involves investing in myself knowledge-wise, including being mindful of who and what I listen to. *Continuous progress forward* is my other mantra. Each year, I have a budget for how much I plan to spend on conferences that heighten my intellectual awareness or that will help me grow into whatever topic or area I goal set for the year. It is not selfish to love oneself and make your happiness a priority. It is preservation. Nurturing you means actively, on a daily basis listening to what innately fuels you and continuously refilling your tank.

Establishing Boundaries

"Boundaries define us. They define what is me and what is not me. A boundary shows me where I end and someone else begins, leading me to a sense of ownership."

Henry Cloud

Anything of value is worth protecting. This is the basis for the existence of alarm companies (manufacturers and monitoring companies), insurance companies, the concept of safe deposit boxes, etcetera. When we value things outside of ourselves, we go to means (sometimes extreme) to protect it. The same concept should apply to us as people. One arm of protection is to establish a set of boundaries that protects the inner core of who we are. For me this means that there are certain behaviors I do not tolerate (cursing, disrespect, dishonor, lies, etcetera). It means I now set the standard of how I want to be treated. Establishing boundaries for me also means I have the privilege of choice—I have the right to say no (with or without reason). I may ask opinions for the primary purpose of edification, but in the end I have the choice to say no. Boundaries may look different for each person. The common factor is that your inner voice should be speaking louder than the voices external to you. Boundaries are important. Boundaries are healthy. Boundaries are a means of protecting the authentic you.

Mindful Thoughts

"Emancipate yourselves from mental slavery.
None but ourselves can free our minds."

The Legendary Bob Marley

I am a Jamaican. I love various genres of music, but reggae music holds a special place in my heart. I admire Bob Marley—the singer, the songwriter, the musician, the man. I have cocktails in our restaurant named after him (and Rita Marley as well). I was three years old when he died. But although Bob Marley the man is no longer living, his music has transcended his life and serves as an inspiration to not just me but countless others. My goal for this book is the same—to live on long after I have left this earth and to be a source of inspiration for others. One of my favorite Bob Marley songs is titled "Redemption Song." It is a song of triumph. Within this song Bob notes that "none but ourselves can free our minds," which is a quote paraphrased from the famous Marcus Mosiah Garvey, but which Bob uses to suggest that we have within ourselves what we need to break free from our thoughts that are holding us in bondage. Our whole life is in our heads, that delicate spot between our ears—our minds. Our thoughts create our habits, ultimately defining the life we live. For me this means I speak positively to myself about myself at all times. It means "I can't" is replaced by "I shall," as long as it is something I want to do and is within the bounds of my integrity. It means that whenever negative thoughts creep in, I make every effort to replace them with positive thoughts. When we free ourselves from self-sabotaging thoughts, we release our capacity to be our authentic selves. One sure way to achieve this is to find a reason bigger than yourself and allow it to propel you into uncovering your purpose. Warning! You will have to leave your comfort zone—the physical and mental limitations, do something new, do something unimaginable, something you previously thought you could not conquer, celebrating the small wins along the way to keep your confidence intact, and remembering that at times when you fail, it is just the Divine steering you in the right direction.

Seek Wholeness

"Seek wholeness, not balance for it is through wholeness that you are at your best version of you."

Georgia Wolfe-Samuels

When I think of wholeness, I think of showing up in the fullness of my being in every scope of my life—as a mother, a wife, a woman, an employee, a business owner, a sister, a daughter, a friend. Within this scope I am not comparing myself or trying to be anyone else but me. It also means not overextending myself or operating from a checklist, but instead being mindful of how I spend my time, seeking to be fully present in whatever the task or event is at any given time. This can be challenging with the different hats I wear simultaneously. But all these hats hold a special significance in my life for which I am grateful. I work from my present, which is oftentimes difficult because I am naturally a planner. I do not allow myself to regurgitate past negative experiences, I leave that for the cows. When I show up as my whole self, I find that each experience holds greater meaning, and my response through these experiences is of more significance and intent. This requires intention, self-discipline, and constant envisioning of who I am and showing up as her.

Success as Defined by Her

"When things change inside of you,
you show up and respond differently."

Georgia Wolfe-Samuels

Be Fruitful

"Be fruitful and multiply" is a common phrase I hear mostly in a biblical sense over the years. It is part of our purpose here on earth, and allows us to share in God's glory. I believe this command extends beyond procreation. The Bible tells of the many things created by Him. But God did not physically create the airplane, or the basketball, or the mirror, or the hair comb or the cars, or the creative cuisines we consume, or the plethora of other things we use or partake in in our daily lives. He created mankind and uniquely equipped us each with talents and a purpose to create these masterpieces, each serving a specific purpose ... serving others outside of ourselves. Each invention is the product of a human mind just like yours and mine. Our job is to unveil our gifts and talents and be brave enough to release it.

The preceding chapters detail the mighty work that God performed in me to course correct my path. In Part II of this memoir I hinted on the conception of our latest business venture (at least at the time this memoir was written)—the opening of our Caribbean restaurant. I don't believe I could have successfully accomplished this endeavor in the state of mind I was in prior to my disruption or attain my current level of success without the opportunity to reflect and redefine my thoughts as a result of the disruption. I am now a strong believer that our net worth is directly interconnected to our self-worth. To clarify, this does not mean that our self-worth is attached to anything outside of us, because our worth cannot be measured in any tangible form. Instead, it means that what you focus your thoughts on is what will expand in your life. When we believe we are worthy of more, we are motivated to pursue actions that will allow us to accomplish that which we desire. The disruption was to clear the path and allow for the true essence of who I was to freely flow alongside with my husband into the creation of our first restaurant. I was able to leverage my skill sets into all aspects of this venture—from the concept, the interior design (my absolute favorite part of the process), business plan, staffing attire, and all that which was required to open our doors, and keep it running, and to stay afloat even during the COVID-19 pandemic. Knowing, believing in, and appreciating my V.A.L.U.E. created tangible results. Appreciating my value empowered me to refine my own personal brand, gave me courage and confidence to venture into entrepreneurship, and to strategize and pivot when needed.

Remain in the Vine

He is the Vine and the Truth. I am Iridescence, created in His image, purposefully and wonderfully made. He commands us to "remain in [Him] as [He] also remain in [us]. No branch can bear fruit by itself; it must remain in the vine. Neither can you bear fruit unless you remain in [Him]." (John 15:7) (NIV) Redefining me allowed for room to dream bigger, and oh boy, are those dreams big! So big that they scare me at times. But the redefined me confidently believes that with Him and through Him, these dreams will manifest. In that truth I stand tall, purposed, and fully poised to change the life of others. The final personal mantra I will leave you with—*I am healed from my past wounds, empowered for impact and restored into my authentic self.* You can be too—you are one thought away from a completely different life—it starts with learning to understand whose and who you are and eradicating what is not authentic to you. Assess the symptoms that show up as problems in your life, and commit to doing the foundational work necessary to eradicate the coping mechanisms with the ultimate goal to experience true healing. Choose your thoughts carefully. Do the work and know that when adversity or fear strikes (because it will at some point), you can respond in **POWER** (Perspectives. Optimism. Wisdom. Empathy. Respect), all the while staying true to the authentic you. Once you have redefined yourself never stop reinventing yourself, forever expanding your dimensions and horizons. You have a decision to make. Redefine your perception of who you are. Your highest and most powerful self is waiting.

Be H.E.R.
Healed. Empowered. Restored.

Pause † Reflect

- The Redefined Her is confident.
- The Redefined Her elevates her self-worth from within, not from external factors.
- The Redefined Her dreams bigger, believing she can manifest that which she desires.
- The Redefined Her establishes and honors her boundaries.
- The Redefined Her is fruitful in all aspects of her life.
- The Redefined Her is more than enough.
- The Redefined Her is empowered to dream and manifest her dreams.
- The Redefined Her acts and responds from a place of **POWER** (Perspectives. Optimism. Wisdom. Empathy. Respect).
- The Redefined Her shows up as her authentic self, from a place of wholeness.

Epilogue

In all my years of conventional schooling—preschool through graduate school, I have never taken a class or was ever provided a manual that taught me how to navigate the traumatic walks of life. I learned through my experiences, each one leaving an impression that would impact how I responded to the world. Within *Redefining Her* I use my raw and personal story with hope that tales of my journey will encourage and lead you to unveil you in your truest form, to change your self-perception, to give you strength and empower you to define and design new possibilities in every facet of your life. I share my highs and my lows as evidence that it is possible to heal from the traumas and struggles we have endured. *Redefining Her* is about transformation, the shifting of our perspective of ourselves and allowing for the clearing of all that is not authentically us to make room for the manifestation of our dreams. *Redefining Her* is about progression, requiring ongoing action as we continue to grow, unencumbered by other's opinions or expectations of us. *Redefining Her* is a passageway to a new you, a version of you that is confident, a version of you that knows her worth, a version of you who knows that you are more than enough, the version of you that responds to the world in **POWER** (Perspectives. Optimism. Wisdom. Empathy. Respect), the version of you that shows up as the highest and best version of you.

Within these pages I have shared with you my journey with hopes to inspire you to embrace and find the gems in your past story—disruption and all, and to empower you to show up authentically for all future chapters. *Redefining Her* is just the beginning. Life will continue to challenge you, but I encourage you to ground your perspectives through His lens, a vantage point that can only be achieved if you remain in the vine. If this memoir empowers one woman with the bravery and guidepost to redefine her *(thoughts, image, finances, dreams, standards, etc.),* and to transform her reality, responding to life as the highest version of her most powerful self, then my blotches, wounds and resulting scars were well worth it. The choice is yours.

- You and only you can manage your thoughts.

- You and only you can control how you respond to your thoughts.

- You and only you can control how you respond to other's opinions and expectations of you.

- You and only you have the choice to debunk thoughts and situations that no longer serve you.

- You and only you, with the right mindset can transform your obstacles into strengths.

- You and only you can decide what version of you shows up.

- Life is about being authentically you. I dare you to be trusting enough to believe in yourself. The world is waiting for the authentic version of you to show up. Be Her fearlessly!

Acknowledgments

I am humbled and forever grateful to share my transformative journey with you. But where would I be today if not for His grace. My Redefine Her journey began long before I penned this book and will continue to advance long after this book finds its way into your hands, as God strategically dismantled who I thought I was, and allowed me to embrace who I am and who I am becoming. To Him I will be forever grateful.

To my daughter Monique who served as my number one cheerleader except for moments when I had to venture off alone for a writing sabbatical, I thank you for your understanding and for allowing me the space to focus, for reading and critiquing my works, and for continuously cheering me on way before I wrote the first word. I am so blessed to call you my daughter.

To my husband Dwight, I thank you for your sacrifice to help me make this dream come through. Thank you for understanding how important this project is to me and for allowing me the time, space and solo trips I needed to bring it to life. I love you with my entire being. Thank you for doing life with me.

To my sister Meggie, thank you for being my ride or die and for giving me your blessing to tell my truth. I am forever grateful for your daily calls, for your encouragement, for your honest opinions.

To my brother Robert, thank you for being my rock.

To all my sister-friends, mentors, therapist, and coaches too many to name, I am forever indebted to you for your prayers, encouragement, and insights, it was a blessing to journey through the disruption, the redefining process and the fruits thereof with you. You are all true friends.

To my team, my publisher and coach Mrs. Ardre Orie, my editors, project managers and design team, I deeply appreciate and thank you for guiding and leading me through this purpose project, continuously telling me "You have a story to tell Queen" and guiding me through the process to tell my story. Thank you for your brilliance and for every opportunity you gave me to learn from you.

About the Author

Mrs. Georgia Wolfe-Samuels is a multifaceted woman living life on her own terms. She is a mother, a wife, a speaker, a redefine her strategist, an author, a CPA, a restaurateur, an entrepreneur, but most importantly, a child of God who decided to answer to the name the Divine called her—Iridescence! She is passionate with a powerful drive to mentor women and girls with hopes of infecting their world with possibilities so they can respond to life with courage and personal power. Her life's pursuit is to use every part of her journey and who she is to love, inspire, motivate, and empower other women suffering from self-doubt and fear, propelling them into their God-given place of self-worth, purpose, and showing up as the highest version of themselves. She is passionate about entrepreneurship and female empowerment with a desire to make self-love go viral.

As an author and mentor, she uses her life of transparency via her writing and speaking platforms to guide women from a relatable yet spiritual perspective. Her literary works include the children's title *I Forgive You Daddy; I Love You Anyway*, and her memoir *Redefining Her*. She resides in the suburbs outside of Atlanta, Georgia with her husband, daughter, and goldendoodle Duke.

The Beginning of Our Connection

You can connect with Georgia Wolfe-Samuels via the following platforms:

- Instagram, Facebook and Twitter @Georgia Wolfe-Samuels
- Website: www.georgiawolfesamuels.com
- Email: GeorgiaWolfeSamuels@gmail.com

Redefining Her Notes

CPSIA information can be obtained
at www.ICGtesting.com
Printed in the USA
LVHW082146050921
697037LV00017B/133